Early Barefootz

Other books
by Howard Cruse

Wendel
Dancin' Nekkid with the Angels
Wendel on the Rebound

by

Howard Cruse

FANTAGRAPHICS BOOKS

FANTAGRAPHICS BOOKS
7563 Lake City Way N.E.
Seattle, WA 98115

Edited and designed by Howard Cruse.
Typesetting by Gil Jordan.
Color separations by Rayson Films.

First Fantagraphics Books edition: December, 1990.
1 3 5 7 9 8 6 4 2

ISBN: 1-56097-052-9 Printed in the U.S.A.

Contents

Preface

Comics readers who've gotten to know me through my *Wendel* comic strips of the 1980s may be unaware that another Howard Cruse once existed, who spent the 1970s drawing underground comix about a cute little guy named Barefootz and the cockroaches, friends and frogs with whom he shared his life.

Those *Barefootz* comix were as different from *Wendel* as night is from day. I'm different, too. I was a callow kid in those days, just learning how to be a cartoonist. Nevertheless there are people in the world who got hooked on *Barefootz*. They didn't care that its big-eyed, friendly look was an anomaly within the belligerently hostile or sardonic world of underground comix. Some of them have been more loyal to *Barefootz* over the years than I've been myself.

Gary Groth of Fantagraphics decided a few years ago that these early *Barefootz* strips of mine should be pulled together into a book. It's taken time for us to get down to the task, but if we were going to do the deed at all, this seems to be the year to do it. After all, Barefootz is hitting his twentieth birthday.

Or at least that's one way to look at it. Technically speaking, *Barefootz* didn't see print until 1971, but I've put the dates 1970–73 on the cover of this volume because I actually started drawing comic strips about the character a year before his official University of Alabama debut. Meanwhile, picky chronologists may notice that some of the pages in this book were actually published in 1975. But these were drawn before 1973 had ended; they just lived in a drawer for two years until the dust settled from the Supreme Court's 1973 obscenity ruling. Other pages, including the twelve-page story "Suffering Celeste," have never been published until now, but have been copyrighted at some point along the way. So be warned that the dates on copyright notices may not always be as informational as you might think.

I've tried to assemble a volume that conveys a general feel for the way my comic strip progressed. For both practical and aesthetic reasons you won't find every *Barefootz* episode ever drawn, but a generous selection of the early strips and practically all the later ones are here. Perfect chronological accuracy is impossible, unfortunately, because in the beginning I kept few records, having no idea during the 1970s that anything like this book would ever happen. Maybe in another twenty years some crazed graduate student will perform the useless task of putting everything in order. In the meantime, there's one quite conscious misordering I'll warn you about: I've concluded this volume with "The Eclipse," even though I drew that story before drawing "Suffering Celeste" and the *Paperman* strips. I plead editorial license. "The Eclipse" makes a better ending for a book.

Two final notes:

In my introduction I tell of the numerous LSD trips I took when *Barefootz* and I were young. The fact that within the body of that essay I not only fail to exhibit any remorse for those drug experiments but even characterize them as creatively and personally beneficial may leave a few eyebrows raised.

Lest they stay that way too long and result in permanent disfigurement, I've appended a short afterword to this book in which I try to clarify my current attitudes toward the psychedelic experience. These reflections are there for those who are interested, but you don't have to read them to laugh at the cockroaches.

Finally, it's sad that I must say this in order to ease the minds of the satirically tin-eared people of the world, but I don't want to add to our nation's distress any more than I have to. The opening words of "Cream of the Genes" are a joke. Neither Captain Kangaroo, Bunny Rabbit, Mister Moose, nor the beloved Mister Green Jeans has ever volunteered any words of praise for this or any other *Barefootz* story.

So rest easy. Your children are safe.

Howard Cruse
August 1990

Acknowledgments

I'm now going to attempt something formidable: I'm going to try to thank everyone who during the last twenty years has offered concrete help to me in the creation and perpetuation of the *Barefootz* series. Given the unreliability of my memory, it's inevitable that I will forget one or more people who clearly should be part of this list; for such lapses I apologize in advance. There are also those who have helped indirectly, by reviewing *Barefootz* in the comics press or by simply offering the moral support that keeps a cartoonist going. Though your names don't appear here, I'll always appreciate your contributions.

Getting specific now: I'm deeply grateful to:

Gene Crutcher, who helped with research for this book and who, along with his wife Bettie, ran Birmingham's legendary Crutcher Books during the '60s and early '70s, where anything I ever published was always stocked, where local artists and writers were always treated as celebrities, where traveling literary figures were automatically offered restroom wall space for their signatures and graffiti, and where anyone who walked in the door was provided with intellectual argumentation upon request;

Julie Brumlik, who volunteered the services, always gratis, of her Manhattan typesetting company, Scarlett Letters, whenever type was needed for my underground comix;

Jennifer Camper, who made this collection economically feasible by pulling dozens of Velox prints from my ancient negatives without charging a penny for her labor;

Bob Carney, the photographer who took the shot of Don that became *Barefootz*'s "flying figure";

Steve Ringgenberg, who has graciously allowed me to include in this book the "Suffering Celeste" exchange from his 1986 *Comics Journal* interview with me;

Denis Kitchen, publisher of Krupp Comic Works/Kitchen Sink Press, who gave *Barefootz* its first national exposure, who stayed loyal when its detractors attacked him for doing so, and who has helped my cartooning career on too many occasions to mention here;

Despina Vodantis, who made a place for *Barefootz* in the University of Alabama *Crimson-White*; Ken Forbes, Jr., who did the same as publisher of *The Alternate*; John Berger, Lee Marrs, and Mal Warwick, proprietors of the Alternative Features Service, who for a time syndicated *Barefootz* to underground newspapers across the land; H. Randall Williams, editor of *The Paperman* in Birmingham, who gave *Barefootz* new life when it looked like the Supreme Court might have killed underground comix; the late Stephen T. Jerrell and Elizabeth Jerrell Flott, who extended my comic strip's life when *The Paperman* folded by including it in *Birmingham After Dark*;

Stan Lee, the Marvel Comics publisher who thought an underground/Marvel hybrid like *Comix Book* was worth a try and thus put my characters in 7-Elevens for the first time; Jim Shooter, former editor-in-chief at Marvel, who without hesitation honored my 1982 request that all rights to my *Comix Book* contributions be transferred from Marvel to me; Deni Loubert, who in 1985 published the Renegade comic book called *Barefootz—the Comix Book Stories*;

Gary Groth of Fantagraphics Books, who decided several years ago that there should be a book-length *Barefootz* collection and who hung in there; Kim Thompson, my production liaison at Fantagraphics; Mike Friedrich of Star*Reach Productions, who took care of the business part;

Jerome K. Lanning, lawyer and fellow graduate of Indian Springs School, who offered legal counsel and did the paperwork, all free of charge, that established the limited partnership called Woofnwarp Productions, a partnership which in turn made it possible for a cartoonist with no money to publish his first solo comic book;

The Woofnwarp Investers, who backed *Barefootz Funnies* #1 in 1985, namely: Dennis Covington; Hubert A. Grissom; Steve Pennington; Innes and Ouida Tartt; and James M. White III. I should add that the motives Jerry Lanning and the aforementioned others had for investing money and energy in my career ranged from friendship to "old school ties" to the simple desire to give a struggling artist his break. No assumptions should be made that any of them knew of or would be inclined to endorse my LSD experiments or my opinions about drugs or other lifestyle issues. (Though at least a couple did and would—hee hee!—and they know who they are!)

Finally, I'd like to offer special thanks to:

Don Higdon, who dreamed along with me the dreams from which *Barefootz* grew, and who cheerfully gave his blessing to my introduction to this book, waving away with heedless abandon my offer to change his name ("My life is an open book," he says—and now that's literally true);

Ed Sedarbaum, my lover of eleven-plus years, who has demonstrated the forebearance of a saint by offering editorial help and advice unstintingly as I wrote glowingly about a former relationship.

This book
is dedicated to
Denis Kitchen
for obvious reasons.

Introduction

At left: Don. Above: me.

Don Higdon was a student at Birmingham-Southern College when we met, a nineteen-year-old sophomore majoring, as I had during my own time at the same college, in theatre. He was a slender guy with riveting blue eyes and fine blond hair. He was an actor.

Unlike some actors, he was quiet on first meeting. I briefly misread his reserve as blandness, but quickly learned better when he began introducing me to the many levels of his funny, philosophical personality. In certain ways he'd just begun to puzzle out who he was. As a matter of fact, he's sworn he didn't realize he was gay until he developed a crush on me, considered my gender, and drew the appropriate conclusion.

I met him at an LSD party in October of 1969. I was tripping in an apartment near the campus along with a group of my friends and other assorted Birmingham acidheads when this young man, whom I'd noticed around the campus but never exchanged more than pleasantries with, squatted near me on the floor, braced a sketch pad on his knee, and began drawing a portrait of my right shoe. He had a gift for likenesses and captured my Hush Puppy perfectly.

We chatted later in the evening when our hallucinations were on the wane and found we had much in common. In the weeks that followed we did more talking, tripping and bonding, and in the course of it fell in love. Come January, we moved in together.

Our apartment was on the city's west side, a few blocks from Birmingham-Southern's green, hilly campus. We had a living room, kitchen, bath, and two bedrooms joined by a hallway. Since we needed only one of the bedrooms for sleeping and making love in, we decided that the other would be my studio. Not that I had the luxury of installing myself there for a full-time artist's life. It was my art department job at a local television station that was supporting me, not any cartoons I might turn out at home.

Our apartment was not in the best of repair, but Don and I accepted its drawbacks with good humor. Though we grumbled the time that a heavy rainstorm propelled the muck from our backyard gully into the living room, we were able to see an object lesson in nature's invasion of our living space—something about the supremacy of the River of Life over humankind's fragile interpolations. (I tended back then to see metaphors readily in life's passing moments. Not just metaphors, but *cosmic* metaphors. You could get wise fast doing those psychedelic drugs!)

LSD (and the other hallucinogens of choice among my crowd: mescaline and psilocybin) had been a big part of my life since they hit the BSC campus back in the spring of 1968, my last term before graduation. I was away living up north for a year thereafter, but Birmingham's acid culture was still going strong when I came back south, and Don was part of it. Don and I did less partying with large groups, though, once we discovered each other. We began looking for opportunities to trip quietly, just the two of us. Sometimes with music playing and sometimes in silence we'd traipse merrily or gravely through the corridors of our individual minds, occasionally issuing bulletins about aspects of ourselves we had discovered. Often we drew pictures. Strange ones. I mulled over comic-strip ideas or scenarios for plays. Don constructed biographies for the characters he was slated to portray on the stage. We also did a lot of dreaming and strategizing about the future. It was a creative time.

One of our favorite tripping places was the large walk-in closet in the hall. We screwed "black lights" into the outlet so that we could sit on the floor and watch our Day-Glo posters shimmer. Sprawling in the purple darkness, we would meditate on surreal drawings of dragons, mystic vistas, and the paradoxes of M. C. Escher. The posters would become windows through which fantastic alternative worlds would beckon. It was this special retreat of ours that I had in mind when I drew Barefootz sighing, "I always wind up keeping my prettiest windows in the closet."

Looking back, I can't imagine that I'd have created *Barefootz* had Don Higdon not been in my life. Not that Don was the model for Barefootz. Don had ambition, something of which Barefootz could never be accused. And I was even less cut from Barefootz's cloth.

I think I *wanted* to be Barefootz, though. Back then. I didn't want to lead Barefootz's life, knocking around an apartment having conversations with bugs, but I wanted to have within me Barefootz's effortless acceptance of things. I'd grown up battered by anxiety; living with Don, inner peace seemed almost attainable. Could it be possible, I sometimes asked myself, to fight the battles of an artist's life while maintaining serenity within one's soul? It's unlikely I would ever have asked a question so audacious had I not, for a while, tasted a life that *almost* had that balance.

Both in *Barefootz* and in *Tops & Button*, my other cartoon series of that period, I was forever trying to capture the state of grace, the sense of underlying pastoral calm amid comic absurdity, that I often felt in my everyday life with Don and in the best moments of the acid trips we shared.

Don and I laughed a lot. Even as we muddled along with the same cranky complaints as anyone else, we simultaneously stood outside Planet Earth shaking our heads benignly at the follies of the creatures running crazily about on its surface. I should add that ours was a stance toward life that in the long run I found wanting. It was too safe and uninvolved. There's comedy, to be sure, in human foibles like vanity, selfishness, and self-deception, but the pain such foibles generate when pushed to cruel extremes cannot be indulgently accepted, or else the human conscience itself will become a joke. Still, experience happens on different levels, and *Barefootz*'s worldview has validity on some of the deeper ones. I may wave placards angrily at political demonstrations today, but I think I'd teeter more dangerously near the edge of despair had I never perceived, along with Barefootz, that "there's a garden in the middle of this comic strip."

An aspect of *Barefootz* that's often been remarked upon is its "innocence." This quality was particularly noticeable in the context of underground comix, where cynicism and aggression were preferred.

I had earned my right by 1970 to celebrate innocence. As a child, before I could have put such a concept as gayness into words, I knew instinctively that I was different from others and that sooner or later the world would punish me for it. I approached adulthood with dread, persuaded by a drumbeat of smirking insinuations that my humanity was irretrievably compromised. Between 1966, the year of my coming out, and the autumn when I met Don, I had put most misgivings about my gayness behind me. But deep within me a few old voices from childhood lingered, whispering that there could be no honor in any love that I felt, that nature had misfired when it made me. Then, during an acid trip in November 1969, reality broke through.

Our friend Caryl had loaned us her apartment for the weekend, which was a big help since neither Don nor I was living alone at the time. We dropped our acid in midevening and within an hour we were off.

My cathartic moment came early in the trip, during the first cascade of hallucinations. Don and I were sitting facing each other, each lost in his own swirl of experience, too far gone at that point to communicate verbally.

As my eyes drifted across the contours of Don's face, a weird, trilling voice filled the air. A record was playing in the next room. Tiny Tim, his falsetto in full throb, was singing "Welcome to My World."

Suddenly my lingering anxieties about gender ambiguity were triggered. My normal ability to accept Tiny Tim on his own quirky terms was undermined as the LSD swept me into the dark areas of my consciousness that still felt betrayed by nature, that still gave credence to the old messages from childhood about the primacy of machismo and the inherent emptiness of a faggot's love.

My throat tightened. I became tense and afraid. For a moment Don's face took on a cast both threatening and sickly. The room felt as artificial and stale as powder caked too thickly onto greasepaint. *What was I doing there?*

But then a dam broke within me and a flood of light poured through my dark passageways. Don's face came furiously alive.

Like bubbles breaking the surface of boiling water, one face replaced another. An old face changed into a young one, then became old again. The transformations accelerated: skin colors darkened and lightened as though racial heritage were a mere trick of lighting. Wrinkles came, then vanished; hair lengthened and shortened; bone structure expanded and contracted with breathtaking fluidity. The shell of flesh that normally encased and limited him, defining Don as a being both spacially separate from other humans and distinct from them in bearing and gender, dissolved before my eyes, leaving me struck with his spiritual link to *all* the people of this planet—the women as well as the men. And I realized that when the face I saw was female, it was no less the Don I loved than when it was male.

During all of this the still, blue eyes at my vision's center didn't change. A strong, secure, comforting presence, they smiled through the rippling hallucinations and kept me anchored.

I began to cry. My knot of self-doubt, buried for so long, broke loose and floated out of me, carried easily by the flood of light. I felt natural to the core, safe in the embrace of those eyes. I could see clearly that gender was irrelevant. It's the soul that loves—not the plumbing.

To finally learn, after all my years of pain, that heaven smiled no less on my rigid dick than it did on the rigid dick of the heterosexual down the street, was a transforming experience. I claim and treasure without apology the innocence that came to me in that moment. The innocence may or may not have made for good cartoons, but I made the best use of it that I could.

An hour or so after that particular cleansing of my psyche (or maybe it was five minutes; time works differently on acid), Don and I realized that we were hungry. Steering our bodies like ships through the sea of psychedelia, we came upon a kitchen. A strangely unfamiliar kitchen. Oh, yes, we remembered after a moment of stoned confusion—it was *Caryl's* kitchen; this was *Caryl's* place we were tripping in.

We explored the kitchen in search of food. The kitchen cabinet had cereal in it. Just what we needed: a box of Sugar Corn Pops with Guy Madison portraying Wild Bill Hickok on the front. We found bowls, lobbed the dumb little kernels into them, added the cool milk that Caryl had left for us in the fridge, and began spooning the crunchy sweet puffballs into our mouths. *Thank you*, our taste buds responded. *Thank you*, our stomachs said. Eating felt so wonderful that we began to laugh, first with delight at the fun of being fed, then at our silliness for guffawing over two bowls of cereal.

And we fell into a fantasy that we were actors in a television commercial for Sugar Corn Pops, one of those TV ads that dramatize the sheer happiness that comes with consumption of a client's product. And surely this must have been the most maniacal of all such ads: two naked hippies, their pupils spinning like pinwheels, shoveling spoonfuls of aerated grain into their gullets while giggling so helplessly that they could barely stay upright in their chairs.

Who needed a voiceover? The image said it all.

A lot of the *Barefootz* strips I drew during the 1970s were about nothing more lofty than the amusement value in a box of Sugar Corn Pops. Life is full of small comic moments. Sometimes we don't notice that they're comic, because they don't come with punchlines attached. But the humor is there. And they're worth drawing comic strips about.

What fascinated me was how transcendental episodes like my epiphany with Don can coexist, comfortably and often unnoticed, alongside the Sugar Corn Pops moments. Underneath the mundane bedsprings of our life, Glory lurks.

The wallboard underneath the kitchen sink in our first apartment had rotted away before Don and I moved in. More seasoned renters would have spotted this gaping hole and demanded that it be mended before the lease was signed. But we were young and impetuous apartment hunters and took possession with only a quick look around.

Obviously, cockroaches don't require so yawning a portal to gain entrance to a dwelling, but the great doorway under our sink must have made our neighborhood roaches feel especially welcome. They came fast and brought all of their friends.

Had we called an exterminator and repaired the hole quickly, we might have stemmed the tide before it got totally out of hand. But we were happy-go-lucky, unfastidious sorts, and we let the matter ride.

In fact, we were held in check for more than a few months by the attitude of delight and wonder that LSD tends to encourage toward all living things, however humble. Albert Schweitzer—at least in this one regard—would have been proud of us. God had made cockroaches as surely as God had made us, we believed. Learning to accommodate ourselves to their presence instead of crushing them underfoot should be enriching as a spiritual discipline.

So for a time (and it was a time that eventually came to an end, I must admit—but I think I'll spare you that ugly tale of carnage) Don and I accepted the presence in ever-mounting numbers of our little roach friends. One of my own strategies for neutralizing the disgust I'd been conditioned to feel was to meditate on the little beasts as they caught some sun next to my coffee cup. If they would stay still long enough, I'd grab my Rapidograph and do a portrait, trying, as I sketched, to look at life from their point of view.

They grew cheeky, once they figured out that Don and I were pacifist patsies. Throwing caution to the wind, they would strut across the arms of our chairs within inches of our fingers, twitching their antennae at us and smirking.

For a time a "yellow submarine" also lived in our kitchen: a hollow, three-dimensional plywood replica, painted a bright goldenrod and roughly thirty inches in length, of the magic vessel the Beatles sang about. It was built as a prop for a 1969 experimental BSC theatre production called *Opus 1*. When the show's run was over and the set was struck, Don was allowed to take it home as a souvenir. We placed it next to the window that overlooked our backyard gully.

Below: the earliest version of Barefootz applies for a job.

Before we knew it the submarine had become a luxury condo for those cockroaches who had grown weary of the seedier ghetto underneath the sink. The prop builder had left its wooden planes imperfectly joined, so that gaps existed through which roaches could easily squeeze. Which they zealously did. Major colonies were soon raising families in the submarine's dark interior. No one could know how many bugs were lurking inside that yellow box at any given time, but we imagined millions. The submarine fairly radiated roach energy.

Were we dismayed? Not seriously enough to take corrective action. Were we intimidated? Yes, we were.

But psychedelic drugs helped us keep our cool. I remember a mescaline trip when we had *Revolver* playing on the turntable and the chorus of "Yellow Submarine" came wafting through the air. The voices of John, Paul, George and Ringo were transmuted into the voices of cartoon cockroaches—a chorus line of them serenading us from within their plywood condo. "We all live in a yellow submarine," sang the funny bugs in the box. "Yellow submarine. . . yellow submarine!"

Those clowns were *born* to be in comic books!

Barefootz was born of a doodle. If memory serves, I first drew him in December of '69. He had five, rather than four, points of hair at inception. His suit and tie were already rumpled upon arrival. His bare feet were gigantic.

I had no idea who the character might be, but I did know instantly that his name was Barefootz. His decision to wear business attire while rejecting shoes intrigued me. It expressed my own conflicted sense of identity. The Magical Mystery Tours I was taking on weekends didn't segue all that smoothly into the mundane demands of Monday-through-Friday survival. Was I the barefooted acid sprite I saw in the mirror on Saturday nights or the neatly turned-out commercial artist who strode through Channel 42's lobby on weekdays?

Below: the world of the squirrels. . .

My first stab at building a syndicated comic strip around Barefootz misfired. Set in an office where free-spirited Barefootz was reluctantly seeking employment, the storyline represented too literal a transcription of my personal malaise. I had in mind an allegory about the subversion of corporate values by a spaced-out flower child. It was an interesting premise, but I made the classic mistake that impatient young artists often make: I tried to force onto paper an idea that had yet to gel in my mind. Though I mailed those hurriedly drawn sample strips to some syndicates, I was lukewarm about them myself, and half expected the cold shoulder they got.

In the meantime, my attention turned to squirrels.

Like *Barefootz, Tops & Button* grew out of an idle sketch. Two vertical lines, to be exact. The edges of a tree trunk, perhaps? I added two holes in the trunk. Squirrel heads emerged. Who were these squirrels? I drew a tall, thin box around the tree and considered the possibilities. Suppose the squirrel on top were to say something and the squirrel on the bottom were to respond. Suppose what they said were to be mildly funny. Could there be a cartoon series in this? A series that might appeal to a mainstream Birmingham audience?

I mulled over practicalities. My squirrels-in-a-tree imagery was pretty simple, graphically speaking. I could knock out six such drawings a week easily, I figured, even on top of my 9-to-5 job. Maybe a corny, unassuming funny-animal panel would actually play in one of our local dailies.

I drew three weeks' worth of samples and made an appointment with Duard LeGrand, the editor of the Birmingham *Post-Herald.* He had been a friend and colleague of my father's years ago. That couldn't hurt.

LeGrand liked my squirrels and immediately recognized the handiness of *Tops & Button*'s vertical format. Newspapers can always use one-column filler. None of the *Post-Herald*'s popular strips would need to be bumped from the comics page to make room for my series; the squirrels could do their thing wherever a hole opened up in the day's layout. LeGrand agreed to launch *Tops & Button* as a daily feature on June 8, 1970. A two-year run ensued.

. . . including a mindfuck installment.

Above: the strip drawn for *Head*.

Tops & Button laid the groundwork for the cartooning approach I'd be using a year later in *Barefootz.* The pastoral feel of it foreshadowed *Barefootz*'s unhurried calm. The dialogue in *Tops & Button* often had a philosophical subtext, as did the conversation and events in *Barefootz.* And like *Barefootz,* when *Tops & Button* was satirical, it was gentle about it. It almost never sneered.

The graphic look of *Tops & Button* also foreshadowed the look of *Barefootz.* The concept of my squirrel series required that each day's panel feature the same long shot of the tree, always seen from its roots to the lowest of its branches. Because the tree's size never varied, neither did the sizes of the characters playing scenes alongside it, who, like actors on a stage, were always seen from head to toe.

I unconsciously brought this visual pattern along when I got the chance to revive *Barefootz.* That happened when, late in 1970, the editor of one of Birmingham's periodic stabs at underground journalism asked if I'd draw a full-page comic strip for his venture. In laying out what was intended to be the introductory episode for a continuing series, I used no changes of perspective and kept to simple, full-body shots in the *Tops & Button* mode. Force of habit was at work.

Later on I gave myself permission to loosen up, but by then I'd learned to appreciate the virtues of a limited palette. Emphasizing dialogue and body language over graphic flash pleased both the playwright and the theatre director in me. When I was in college we had mounted many a play on a bare stage, and in doing so we had observed how the absence of a set can give the words and actions of actors added power. Remembering this lesson, I began consciously looking at *Barefootz* as—in essence if not literally—a bare-stage comic strip.

But 1970 wasn't to be *Barefootz*'s year. *Head,* the underground paper for which my reconstituted *Barefootz* was slated, folded almost before it began. *Barefootz* had to wait until June of 1971 to make its debut.

The Crimson-White Strips

BAREFOOTZ

BAREFOOTZ

Despina Vodantis made it happen. She had been a friend of Don's since they met in the eighth grade at Fairfield Junior High. After graduation Don enrolled at Birmingham-Southern and Despina at the University of Alabama in Tuscaloosa. The two of them kept in touch and, when Don and I became lovers, Despina became my friend as well.

In the spring of '71 Despina won the editorship of the U of A's student newspaper, the *Crimson-White*. She decided to try something novel: she commissioned an original comic-strip series from me.

Barefootz was called into action again. I'm not sure why I thought students at the University of Alabama would be interested in a feature that had no teachers, classrooms, books, football games, finals, frats, or beer. I just plunged ahead and drew the comic strip I was in the mood to draw, a strip full of weirdness, nonsequiturs, surrealism, roaches, and frogs. Despina, bless her heart, let me do my thing freely.

The first *Barefootz* strip appeared on June 14, at the beginning of the university's summer term. Unlike the installments that commenced the following fall, those eight strips published weekly during the summer were a continuing narrative. They depicted the unfortunate fate of a woman named Frances, who got her mind blown by Glory and was never seen again.

Frances paid a heavy penalty for lugging her paranoid sexual baggage into Barefootz's bedroom. Barefootz should have posted a warning sign over his apartment door: *All hope abandon, ye who bring your libidos here.* No punishment of such harshness was ever meted out to Dolly, who joined the *Crimson-White* cast in the fall and stayed for the duration, even though she did transgress, like Frances, by nakedly displaying her erotic obsessions. But even so, no one could accuse me of treating Dolly kindly. She was condemned to suffer the humiliating rejection of her achingly available body for years on end. Indeed, in the earliest installments of the series she was offered up to readers implicitly as an object of

ridicule, as if a tubby woman with yearning in her loins were a brand of ridiculous mutant from whom the pure of heart must surely recoil.

Was this fair? No. Was this sexist? Yes. Intellectually, I counted myself an early convert to feminism, but as a twenty-five-year-old male raised in 1950s and 1960s America, I still had plenty of unconscious male chauvinism to unload. Our culture rewards its comedians for comedy that demeans, and I remained capable in the early '70s of rationalizing my bids for such cheaply gained rewards. (I was even prepared to demean *myself* if I could get a snicker out of it: you'll find more than one fag joke in my strips of this period.)

More than garden-variety sexism was at work, of course, when I set Dolly up for humiliation. Dolly, who was guilty only of healthy lust, bore the brunt of my ancient rages. As an adolescent I'd been in on the bull sessions where guys would parade their sexual bravado, and I knew what was expected of a "real man" should a girl who was ready to "put out" cross his path. But I was gay, so I steered clear of girls who might put my pretenses of heterosexuality to the test. The occasional girls who pushed, as Dolly pushed Barefootz, scared me and made me angry.

The adult cartoonist who was drawing *Barefootz* in the early '70s thought he'd worked through all this stuff. But old stowaway resentments surfaced and crept through my comic strip's back door. They manifested themselves in the way I depicted Dolly, and some female readers eventually called me on my chauvinism. Their objections were unquestionably on target.

But even as I own up to my malfeasance, I'd like to offer a point in my defense. The Dolly who grasped grotesquely for Barefootz in the *Crimson-White* strips was not the Dolly of a later time. Even before feminist criticisms reached my ears I had realized how inappropriate it was to stand outside of Dolly and sneer, and I set about a gradual midcourse correction. Her hyperdrive horniness had already been established, but there's nothing about lust itself to apologize for. I looked at the world through her eyes and found much to identify with. Who of us hasn't known

the pain of unreciprocated passion? Who has never recklessly provoked his or her own humiliation? I certainly have. Dolly's inability to stay cool and conceal her yearnings made me love her. She, in the baldness of her lust, was the opposite of the secret yearner I'd been during my closeted youth, and I admired her for it. She was as helplessly open in the expression of her desires as I had been dedicated to the concealment of mine. It had hurt to hide my feelings. Hooray for Dolly that she didn't!

Though Barefootz remained sexually unavailable, I made sure that he never shunned Dolly. She remained welcome at his side, a peer and pal, for as long as I drew the series. Just because he never slept with her doesn't mean his acceptance of her was less than complete.

But why *didn't* Barefootz sleep with Dolly? For a male to fail to take advantage of a woman's body freely offered was, particularly by underground-comix standards, pretty unbutch!

Was he gay?

That's a question I was asked occasionally by my friends in the early days and even more frequently once I'd told the comics world that *I* was gay. In general, I responded that Barefootz was impervious to worldly temptation because he was not quite *of* this world. As the last of the *Crimson-White* strips suggests, he was perfectly capable of sidling at will right out of our plane of existence. Even when he was in the room with you, should you try to straighten his clothes, as Dolly did once, you could find that you were dealing with ether. Was this the sort of being who might suffer from horniness?

Actually, to point solely to *Crimson-White* episodes begs the question. Barefootz became more "of this world" as time went by (just as, with our lessening use of psychedelics in 1973, Don and I did). But in 1971 he was still too spacey even for me—much less Dolly—to get a handle on. If he was anything, though, my guess was that he was straight.

BAREFOOTZ

BAREFOOTZ

The 1971-72 *Crimson-White* strips straddled the boundary between what was conventional in comic-strip humor and what was freaky. Many had perfectly normal punchlines. Others had no demonstrable connection to linear humor as we know it. My principal running gags—Glory's taste for roach meat and her habit of belching up frogs—must surely have left a few of my college readers shaking their heads. Mine wasn't the most responsible or professional of attitudes: I had only a secondary interest in communicating with *normal* people. I was principally after the university's tiniest minorities: the potheads, acidheads, absurdists and freaks.

I took the most extreme liberties with my "mindfuck" episodes. These were the strips whose first order of business was to disorient. Not only were there no jokes, there was no rationality. I fished for images that, while striking enough to entertain the eye, rewarded the intellect with only the slipperiest intimations of meaning. I wanted to beckon the reader's mind toward the dream state's edge while denying it the safety of sure footing.

I was inspired, of course, by the other underground cartoonists who were engaged in similar explorations. The surrealism of the acid experience was so arresting, for those of us who'd been there, that it was almost impossible not to search for ways to document it.

BAREFOOTZ
by HOWARD CRUSE
©1971 by H. Cruse

?
WHAT'S HAPPENING?
RUN
GRAB THAT
LOOK OUT
EEK
GET UP QUICK
HURRY
CHEESE IT!
CLICK!

I HOPE I DIDN'T INTERRUPT ANYTHING...
CRUSE

BAREFOOTZ
by HOWARD CRUSE
I CAN'T THINK...
I DON'T KNOW WHO I AM!!
©1971 by H. Cruse

I FEEL LIKE I'M IN A COMIC STRIP AND PEOPLE ARE LOOKING AT ME AND SMIRKING!

NOW THE ROOM IS FILLED WITH HORRIBLE HUMAN BEINGS...
AND THEY'RE CRAWLING ALL OVER ME!

©1971 by H. Cruse
HAVE YOU BEEN O.D.-ING ON VITAMINS AGAIN?
Pant
Pant
Pant
CRUSE

BAREFOOTZ
by HOWARD CRUSE
YOU'VE GOT TO STOP EATING THE ROACHES, GLORY!
©1971 by H. Cruse

THE ROACHES ALL SAY THAT THEY'RE AFRAID TO COME OUT IN THE DARK, FOR FEAR THAT THEY MIGHT WANDER UNDER THE BED!...

THEY SAY THAT YOU GRAB THEM AND SWALLOW THEM WHOLE AND TURN THEM INTO COSMIC DUST AND SEND THEM ORBITING AROUND PLANETS IN SOLAR SYSTEMS ENTIRELY DIFFERENT FROM OUR OWN WHERE THEY CAN'T WRITE LETTERS TO THEIR MOTHERS!

YOU'RE GIVING THE ROACHES BAD TRIPS, GLORY!
CRUSE

BAREFOOTZ
by HOWARD CRUSE
YOU'VE GOT TO STOP EATING THE ROACHES, GLORY!
©1971 by H. Cruse

THIS IS THE ROACHES' APARTMENT AS MUCH AS YOURS OR MINE, AND IF WE'RE GOING TO BE HAPPY, WE'RE ALL GOING TO HAVE TO LEARN TO LIVE TOGETHER IN PEACE AND HARMONY!

GRONK! GRONK! GRONK! GRONK! GRONK! GRONK!

DON'T MAKE FROGS AT ME, GLORY!
CRUSE

BAREFOOTZ
by HOWARD CRUSE
IT'S TRUE THAT I'M SEXUALLY FRUSTRATED...
BUT THAT'S NOT MY REAL PROBLEM!

MY REAL PROBLEM IS THAT I'M HUNGRY!

I MEAN, I'M STARVING...
BUT I HAVE TO HOLD IT ALL INSIDE OF ME!

©1971 by H. Cruse
MY LACK OF SEX IS ONLY AN OUTLET!
CRUSE

Here and there on the countercultural landscape were trippers who reported to their friends that they'd "seen God" on acid.

Such reports were rarely accepted at face value, though fellow trippers were less likely than nontrippers to dismiss them out of hand. After all, they'd witnessed some pretty strange things themselves. Even when a listener harbored doubts, a respectful "Oh, wow, that's far out!" was usually enough to move the conversation along. On the whole, the religious experiences of others were like ghost stories and UFO reports: worth a furrowed brow and a shake of the head, but best not proselytized about.

So although Don and I once shared a "white light" flash on psilocybin that has given me plenty to chew on theologically ever since, I'll refrain from asking you to take it seriously. One epiphany per essay is enough. I mention it only because you'll notice intimations of it surfacing periodically in my comix—along with spoofs of the more conventional religious outlooks that were the flip side of my newly discovered cosmology.

Art forever lures you back to the inner places where things get intense. I was a preacher's kid, and religion has always been one of those intense places for me. I arrived at my mid-twenties an agnostic, but psychedelics gave me a new frame of reference. I was forever circling my white-light memory, trying to suggest through pictures what I couldn't say with words.

Once, sometime in 1971 as I recall, I got the idea for a psychedelic poster that would mix the imagery of religion as I had known it when I was growing up, with the ecstatic feelings of spirituality that I had experienced under the influence of psilocybin. The poster would be dominated by the image of a naked male figure with arms outstretched in a position that called to mind Christ on the cross but that could as easily be seen as a sublimely liberated human in flight. I would surround the figure with psychedelia and let the acidheads groove.

There was a problem, though: I wanted the figure drawn in a more realistic style than I felt capable of rendering. I needed photographic reference. Fortunately, Don, who was bearded and had shoulder-length hair at the time, looked quite a bit like the classic Christ from my old Sunday School literature. I recruited Don to be my model.

The staff photographer at Channel 42 agreed to do the shoot. He set up his tripod late one afternoon when the studio was free. Don stripped down to his bathing suit, climbed a ladder, threw his head back, and extended his arms. The shutter snapped and the deed was done. When a print was ready, I converted it into a high-contrast line drawing. In the process I divested Don of his swimwear.

My poster was never printed, but I made alternative use of the drawing of Don in flight. Beginning with "The Eclipse," portions of my flying figure could be seen somewhere in the background of practically every *Barefootz* story. The figure suggested something mysterious and joyous to me. He was a visitor from some other plane of reality, briefly penetrating the *Barefootz* world, but only briefly. In a comic strip populated by cartoony people with huge heads and tiny bodies, he was drastically, provocatively out of place. By his very presence he said, "Don't be *too* sure you know what's going on. It may be something else entirely."

I consider this good advice for any religionist—myself included.

Despina's term as editor of the *Crimson-White*—and *Barefootz*'s life as a college strip—ended in the spring of 1972. But my characters bounced back shortly thereafter in the pages of an underground paper called *The Alternate.*

The Alternate was the baby of Ken Forbes, Jr. Ken was the owner of a record store called Angry Revolt, which was located in Homewood, one of Birmingham's suburbs to the south. As the name he chose for his record store suggests, Ken had a rebellious streak. He felt provoked enough by Birmingham's conservatism to fund yet another underground newspaper for the metropolitan area's youth culture. *The Alternate* had enough legs to survive nearly two years, from April of 1972 (the month of its debut is an estimate: "We were too busy thinking about Peace and Love," Ken says today, "to think about putting dates on the masthead!") until February of 1974.

Ken hired me to spend a couple of nights a week in the balcony of his record store laying out his paper, composing headlines, and doing drawings for filler. As part of the deal I was given space each issue for a half-page installment of *Barefootz.*

This arrangement lasted until September, when Don and I were offered jobs at the Atlanta Children's Theatre. That summer had been a season of change for both

of us: Don had graduated from Birmingham-Southern and I had ended the *Tops & Button* series and quit my job at Channel 42. With Don no longer tethered to the college and with me feeling more committed to my cartooning ambitions than ever before, the two of us were in a mood to move on to the next adventure.

Much would happen during the fifteen months that followed that would radically alter both of our lives. My memory of our exciting departure from Birmingham will always be shaded with sadness, since I know now that we would spend only two autumns together in Atlanta before our relationship would come to an end. Life was forcing us to get more serious about ourselves and our individual futures. Subtle differences in our priorities were beginning to grow more distinct: 1973 saw me becoming more political, while Don's focus on his acting ambitions intensified. The paths of our lives were diverging, and a painful break was coming.

But all of that was to come later; in the fall of 1972 we still had more than a year of shared excitement ahead of us. Our lifestyle had become more sedate with time, I must admit. Our zest for tripping had abated. We'd begun to sense that, after several dozen trips, we'd absorbed most of what psychedelics had to teach us. It's ironic that by the time my comix had begun proclaiming my identity as an unapologetic acidhead to a national audience, my actual drug use was virtually a thing of the past. My best highs now were coming from the comix I was drawing.

I had learned of Kitchen Sink Comix a year or so earlier through a listing Denis Kitchen had placed in the *Writer's Yearbook*. Before leaving Birmingham I sent Denis a batch of the *Crimson-White* and *Alternate* strips I'd done. I heard from him a short time after Don and I had settled into our new Atlanta quarters. Denis liked my *Barefootz* characters and encouraged me to think of Kitchen Sink as a regular market.

By that time I'd gleaned an important insight from my eighty-eight performances as a spear-carrier in *Robin Hood*: my future did not lie in professional acting. Although I did part-time backstage work for an additional three months, Denis's invitation to enlist in the comix underground came when I was hungrier than ever for a full-time cartooning career.

Fired with enthusiasm, I threw myself wholeheartedly into comix. During the months that followed I drew "Tussy Comes Back," "Cream of the Genes," "The Eclipse," and "Suffering Celeste," plus dozens of single-pagers. The Senate Watergate hearings kept me company as I scribbled and stippled. Don was away much of the time, rehearsing for Atlanta projects, doing shows in different cities, chasing down chances to audition. I was happy to stay at home, blissfully absorbed in a world of roaches, frogs, and weirdly shaped humans. Feeling myself on a roll, I anticipated an ever-expanding future in underground comic books. I should have

known the hazards in letting my expectations grow so bold.

In midsummer Denis Kitchen wrote with grim news. His publishing plans were being devastated by fallout from the U.S. Supreme Court's ruling on obscenity that had been handed down in June. Artists still wanted to draw underground comix and readers still wanted to read them, but retailers were afraid to carry them and channels of distribution were fast drying up. Events were forcing Denis to put almost all of his publishing projects on hold. It was unclear whether his company would even survive.

For me it was a bruising plummet. My license to spend whole days drawing had been revoked. I glumly tucked my stack of unpublished *Barefootz* pages in a drawer and started looking for "real" work. Soon I was spending my days operating a photostat camera for a neighborhood commercial art studio.

There was no place to publish the long stories I had already drawn, but I was able during the fall of '73 to keep *Barefootz* alive in a small way. Word reached me in August of a new alternative weekly that had been launched in Birmingham called *The Paperman.* I mailed samples to its editor and was offered a weekly half-page slot. Drawing strips during the evening, I set a sustainable pace for myself and hoped for better times to come.

BAREFOOTZ
by HOWARD CRUSE
MOMMY! THERE'S SOMETHIN' WEIRD UNDER THIS BED!

IT'S GREEN AND IT'S YELLOW AND IT'S ORANGE AND IT'S PURPLE AND IT'S......
©1972 by H. Cruse

SKINCH!

BERNIE..?
FAR OUT
CRUSE

BAREFOOTZ
by HOWARD CRUSE
HERE'S A NICE BOWL OF MILK I'VE POURED FOR YOU, GLORY!

CRUSE

MY MILK BILL'S NOT SO BAD...
IT'S MY BOWL BILL THAT'S BREAKING ME!
BURP!

BAREFOOTZ
by HOWARD CRUSE
I'VE GOT TO GET BAREFOOTZ OFF MY MIND!
CRUSE

I'VE GOT TO COMPLETELY FORGET HE EXISTS!

HI, DOLLY!

YOU'RE NOT HELPING!!
©1972 by H. Cruse

BAREFOOTZ
by HOWARD CRUSE
©1972 by H. Cruse

THONK!

SORRY ABOUT THAT...
PEOPLE WHO ARE SEXUALLY FRUSTRATED TEND TO KICK FROGS!

WHOMP!

YOU THINK FROGS DON'T GET HORNY?
CRUSE

BAREFOOTZ
by HOWARD CRUSE

?

©1972 by H. Cruse
DID YOU KNOW THERE'S A GARDEN IN THE MIDDLE OF THIS COMIC STRIP?
CRUSE

The underground-comix movement for which I created *Barefootz* survived, I'm relieved to say, though its visibility remains diminished. Knocked temporarily to its knees by the Supreme Court obscenity ruling, Kitchen Sink soon regained its footing and, with a mix of classic reprints and the occasional underground title, is viewed today as one of the comics industry's class acts.

Ironically, a prime instrument of salvation for both Kitchen Sink and me in 1974 was Marvel Comics, that giant of the comics mainstream. In his '73 letter warning me of the hard times to come, Denis hinted of negotiations that were currently under way between himself and "a major publisher." A periodical might be in the wind, he wrote, that could provide a new forum for underground cartoonists. By April 1974, the contracts had been signed and Denis wrote again, this time inviting me to contribute *Barefootz* stories regularly to *Comix Book.*

I was single by that time, and the wounds of my lost relationship with Don were raw. But I still had the memory of a yellow submarine, and inside of it cockroaches still danced.

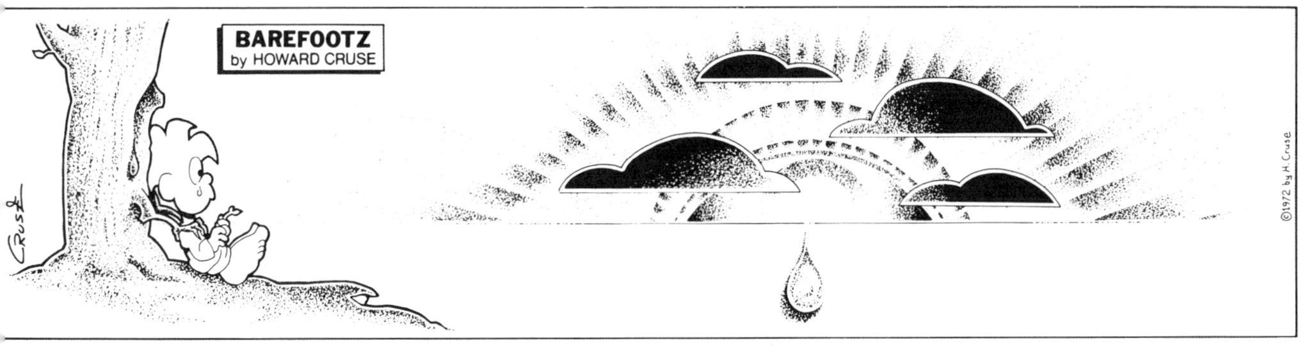

BAREFOOTZ
by HOWARD CRUSE
©1972 by H. Cruse

BAREFOOTZ
by HOWARD CRUSE

WHAP!

ACTUALLY, I PREFER PSYCHO-LOGICAL HUMOR!

BAREFOOTZ
by HOWARD CRUSE
LET ME STRAIGHTEN YOUR SUIT FOR YOU, BAREFOOTZ!
©1972 by H. Cruse

I DON'T SEE HOW YOU CAN STAND TO LOOK SO RUMPLED ALL THE TIME!

I DON'T THINK YOUR CLOTHES ARE THE PROBLEM!

BAREFOOTZ
by HOWARD CRUSE
KA-POW!

WHAT WAS THAT, MISTER BAREFOOTZ?
OH...JUST A PLAN THAT I MADE YESTERDAY!

ANY PLAN THAT I MAKE AUTOMATICALLY SELF-DESTRUCTS AFTER 24 HOURS!
©1972 by H. Cruse

IT HELPS KEEP ME TRANQUIL!

BAREFOOTZ
by HOWARD CRUSE
WHERE WILL YOU BE FOR THE VACATION, BAREFOOTZ?
WHERE-EVER I WIND UP, I SUPPOSE!
©1972 by H. Cruse

WELL, I GUESS IF WE DON'T MAKE IT NOW, WE NEVER WILL!..

!?

BAREFOOTZ
by Howard Cruse
©1972 by H. Cruse

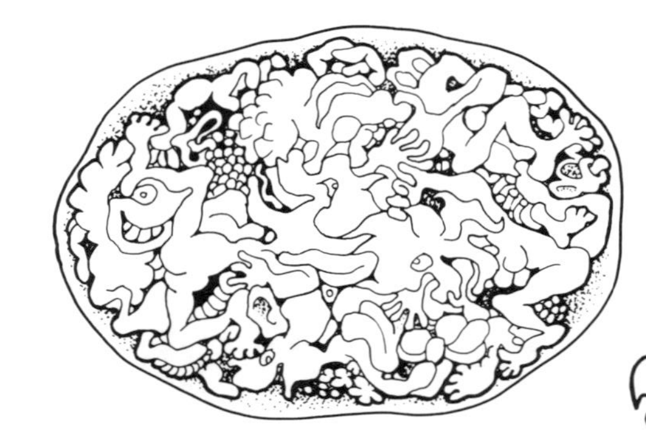

YOU GOT A LEASH FOR THAT THING, BUDDY?

BAREFOOTZ
by Howard Cruse
CLICK!
I JUST LOVE MY CAT!
YOU SHOULD HAVE A PET, BAREFOOTZ!
HAVEN'T YOU MET GLORY?
GLORY?
SHE LIVES UNDER THE BED!
IT'S TOO DARK TO SEE UNDER THERE! WHAT IS SHE?
WELL...THAT'S HARD TO SAY...
BUT SHE'S NOT A CAT!
MY FRITZI IS THE SWEETEST ANIMAL IN THE WORLD!
COOKIES
I CALL HER 'FRITZI' BECAUSE SHE'S SO SENSUAL!
I DON'T THINK I COULD SLEEP WITHOUT FRITZI NUZZLING UP AGAINST ME ON MY PILLOW EVERY NIGHT!
©1972 by H. Cruse
ZAP
WE DON'T TURN OUR FRIENDS' CATS INTO GOLF BALLS, GLORY!
CRUSE

BAREFOOTZ
by Howard Cruse
IT'S THREE O'CLOCK, GLORY!
TIME FOR YOUR MEDICINE!
MMM! IT'S GONNA TASTE SO GOOD...
TONIC
OPEN YOUR LI'L MOUTH WIDE NOW!
GRONK!
GRONK!
GRONK!
GLYERCH!!
DON'T MAKE FROGS AT ME, GLORY!
I KNOW IT CAN'T BE THAT BAD!
©1972 by H. Cruse
BLYUK
CRUSE

BAREFOOTZ
by Howard Cruse
THIS IS A NICE PLACE FOR A WINDOW!
TH' PERFECT POSITION SO THAT I CAN FEEL TH' SUNSET ON MY EARS...
...WHILE I'M LYIN' IN MY FAVORITE SPOT FOR WATCHIN' TH' CEILING!
©1972 by H. Cruse
LOOK AT THAT, FLORENCE!
WHAT AN AWFUL PLACE FOR A WINDOW!
IT RUINS THE DECOR!
...THROWS THE WHOLE ROOM OUT OF WHACK!
ARE YOU RESPONSIBLE FOR THIS, BAREFOOTZ?
AND LOOK WHAT THAT SUN DOES TO MY TAN!
OOO! UGLY FRECKLES!
THERE'S NOTHING UGLIER THAN A FRECKLED ROACH!
AND THE WAY THE LIGHT GLARES ON THE LINOLEUM!
IT'S UNLIVABLE IN THE FRONT WOODWORK!
WHAT'S GOING ON?
ALRIGHT! ALRIGHT!
NOW DON'T GO AND MOVE IT JUST FOR OUR SAKE, BAREFOOTZ...
I ALWAYS WIND UP KEEPING MY PRETTIEST WINDOWS IN THE CLOSET!
CRUSE

BAREFOOTZ
by Howard Cruse
RING!
RING!
HELLO?
2 A.M..?
RING!
©1972 by H. Cruse
PRESS
RING!
RING
HIT!
HIT!
HIT!
RINGRINGRINGRINGRIN
STOMP
STOMP
GRINGRING!
Shake!
Shake!
Shake!
Shake!
RING!
SMASH!
SAY...I'M GLAD YOU DIDN'T LET ME OVER-SLEEP!
CRUSE

BAREFOOTZ
by Howard Cruse
NEVER DATE A PSYCHIATRIST, BAREFOOTZ!
LAST NIGHT DR. BONEYARD INVITED ME OVER FOR A SNACK!
I THOUGHT HE WAS KIDDING WHEN HE STARTED POURING CHOCOLATE SYRUP ON HIS BULLWHIP!
CITY LIMITS
SUDDENLY HE WAS ALL OVER ME...
...STRIPPING ME NAKED AND TAKING LIBERTIES!
IT'S TOUGH FENDING OFF A MAD RAPIST WHO KEEPS SCOOPING WHIPPED CREAM IN YOUR EYES!
FINALLY I GOT THE UPPER HAND...
...BUT NOT BEFORE HE'D RUN MY PANTIES THROUGH A MEAT GRINDER AND DICED MY BRA!
©1972 by H. Cruse
I HAD TO WALK HOME WEARING TWO GRAPEFRUIT HALVES AND A HEAD OF LETTUCE!
SOUNDS LIKE AN EXCITING EVENING!
I DUNNO, BAREFOOTZ...
SOMEHOW IT ALL SEEMED SO CLINICAL!
CRUSE

BAREFOOTZ
by Howard Cruse
CAN I WATCH YOU TRANSCEND YOUR EGO, WALLY?
SURE, BAREFOOTZ!

WOULD YOU MIND HOLDING MY WRIST WATCH?
©1972 by H. Cruse

12:05 AND HOLDING...
OM

VORT
VORT

EXCUSE THAT LAST BIT...I WAS SHOWING OFF A LITTLE!

The Alternative Features Service Strips

In 1972 a handful of *Barefootz* strips were included in the comix packets that were provided by the Alternative Features Service to subscribing underground newspapers.

BAREFOOTZ

by Howard Cruse

TUSSY Comes Back

DON'T OPEN THAT DOOR!

CAN'T YOU SEE WE'RE HAVING A SÉANCE?

PASS THE JOINT, PLEASE...

NOBODY HERE!?
HEADS UP!

WHOA, GODDAMMIT! WHOA!
IT CAN'T BE..!
DOWN, BOY!

TUSSY!
A PERSON COULD GET KILLED...

YOU'VE COME BACK!

YOU'VE COME BACK FROM THE DEAD!
THIS NINNY LOOKS FAMILIAR!

YOU'VE BEEN DEAD FOR THREE WEEKS!
THIS WHOLE PAD LOOKS FAMILIAR!

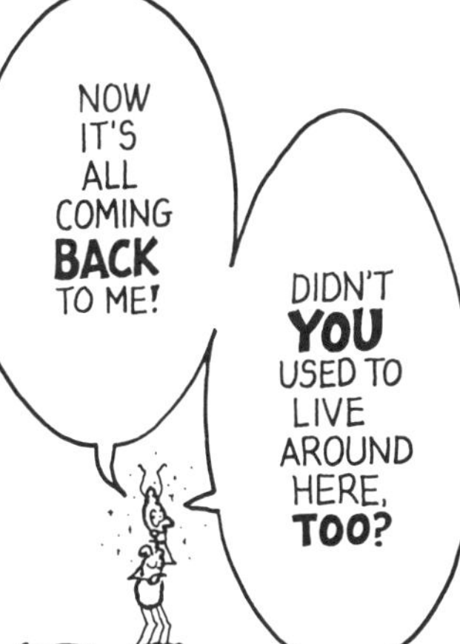
NOW IT'S ALL COMING BACK TO ME!
DIDN'T YOU USED TO LIVE AROUND HERE, TOO?

SURE! I'M BAREFOOTZ! REMEMBER?
WOULD YOU MIND HOLDING ONTO THIS FOR ME?

AN UMBRELLA?
THAT'S WHAT THEY GIVE YOU TO USE 'TIL YOU'VE GOT THE HANG OF HAVING WINGS!

IT'S A BLATANT STEAL FROM SOME DISNEY FLICK, I UNDERSTAND...
WHO IS 'THEY'?
THE ROACH HEAVEN BIG-WIGS, NATURALLY!
2

ROACH HEAVEN?
YEP... THIS IS THE RIGHT ADDRESS!

O.K., KID... WHERE'S THE SÉANCE?

OH! ARE YOU HERE FOR THE SÉANCE?
NO... ACTUALLY- I THOUGHT THIS WAS WHERE THEY HOLD THE MARDI GRAS!

GO AWAY BAREFOOTZ!
WE'RE HAVING A SÉANCE!
TOKE! TOKE!
BUT THERE'S A GHOST HERE TO SEE YOU!

YOU MEAN SHE CAME?

THIS IS FANTASTIC!
I CAN'T BREATHE, I'M SO EXCITED!
...AND ME WITHOUT MY CLEARASIL!
FAR-R-R OUT!

AUNT TUSSY!
YOU!

FORGET IT, BAREFOOTZ!

WELL, WHO WERE YOU GUYS TRYING FOR, ANYWAY?
TALLULAH BANKHEAD?

AS A MATTER OF FACT... YES!
YOU KIDS HAVE GOT A LOT OF NERVE... SMOKING DOPE AT MY FUNERAL!

MAYBE WE MIS-SPELLED 'BANKHEAD.'..
AND TO MAKE IT WORSE- IT WAS MY DOPE!
3

AND THEN, TO MAKE IT EVEN WORSE- YOU DRAG ME BACK HERE!
HERE IN THIS APARTMENT...
HERE WITH THESE WALLS...
HERE WITH THAT CEILING...
HERE WITH THIS FLOOR...
HERE WITH THAT CLOSET...
More on "That Closet" later, Gang!
...AND HERE WITH THIS POOR, STILL-SLIGHTLY-WARM-AND-THROBBING SMUDGE ON THE FLOOR THAT WAS MY MORTAL REMAINS!
(SOB!)
UH-TUSSY... I...
A GENTLEMAN DOES NOT FOLLOW A LADY INTO THE JOHN!
SLAM!
CLICK!
DO GHOSTS TAKE CRAPS?
A VERY PERTINENT QUESTION!
I WONDER IF THEIR PEE IS WARM...
'INTELLECTUAL CURIOSITY' IS TO BE CHERISHED!
I WONDER WHAT KICKING-OFF IS LIKE...
IT PROBABLY DEPENDS ON WHETHER YOU'RE KICKING OR GETTIN' KICKED!
NOW IN AUNT TUSSY'S CASE...
IT'S A LEVELING EXPERIENCE, BOYS...
TELL US ABOUT IT, TUSSY!
TUSSY LEVELS WITH US:
(...IS IT TRUTH—OR AN AFTERFLASH?)
4

"FROM THE TIME I WAS A BABY, I'D BEEN TOLD BY THE OLDER ROACHES WHAT THEY CALLED THE 'FACTS OF LIFE'..."
SOMEWHERE OUT THERE...
...THERE'S A SHOE WITH YOUR NAME ON IT!
RCH-5
"BUT LIKE ALL YOUNGSTERS, I WAS IMPETUOUS..."
THEY'RE ONLY TRYING TO INHIBIT ME!
I DON'T BELIEVE IN 'SHOES'!
"I DISREGARDED THEIR WARNINGS AND LIVED A LIFE OF HEEDLESS ABANDON..."
"UNTIL ONE DAY..."
CREAK!
"...FROM THE CLOSET IN THE HALL—FROM BEHIND THE FAMILY ALBUMS AND BOXES OF OLD VALENTINES AND ABANDONED COOKIES AND 78 R.P.M. RECORDINGS OF MARIO LANZA AND TOMMY CHARLES PLUS THE ONLY EXTANT NUDE PIN-UP OF HARRIET HILLIARD, SOMEWHAT BROWNING NOW AND BURIED UNDER NEARLY A HUNDRED CIRCUS TICKET STUBS—THERE EMERGED..."
"...MY NEMESIS!"
YULP!
IT'S A GIRL, MRS. WALKER, IT'S A GIRL!
A GIRL! A GIRL! A GIR-R-RL!
DON'T WIPE YOUR NOSE ON MY APRON, LOVE...
DO TELL
ME? ON JOHNNY CARSON?
HOWDY DOODY IS NOT EITHER A CATHOLIC!
AM I A TEENAGER YET, MAMA?
NOT TILL YOUR FATHER GETS HOME!
I'D STILL BE A PTERODACTYL IF I WASN'T EXTINCT!
GRITS?
YES GRITS!
BAD KHARMA!
...BUT LOTS OF LITTLE ROACH GIRLS WEAR BRACES, DARLING...
I DON'T CARE IF MY BOOBS ARE CROOKED!
...AND THEN HE LEFT ME FOR A THEORETICAL REDUNDANCY
FUNNY
"Z" IS FOR "ZACHEUS, ZACHEUS, COME DOWN FROM THAT...UH..."
"TREE"
GOO!
MARALYN GOT PREGNANT BY A CRAB LOUSE!
I BET SHE ITCHES!
LOOK, MAMA... I DID IT ON MARY WORTH!
AT LAST... I'M IN LOVE!
JUST DON'T COME RUNNING TO ME!
UGH! YOU'RE ALL WRINKLED!
SHOULD I TELL ON HIM?
CAREFUL... HE'S TIGHT WITH THE MAFIA...
LOOK, MAMA.. I DID IT ON THE TELEVISION!
I'LL NEVER TELL!
YOUR FACE LOOKS DRAWN TODAY!
YOURS DOESN'T!
NO, DEAR... ROACHES DON'T TURN INTO BUTTERFLIES...
STILL BE THERE WHEN YOU'RE MARRIED, DEAR...
"GLORY"? WHAT'S "GLORY"?
HAVEN'T YOU BEEN UNDER THE BED?
...BUT LOTS OF LITTLE ROACH GIRLS' FATHERS ARE FAGGOTS, DARLING...
SPACEY BABY
I'M ONLY FIVE AND I'M ALREADY BORED!
HAVE YOU TRIED GOD?
NEVER BE AN ARTIST!
NO MAN IS AN ISLAND (GIGGLE)
BULL! I KNOW HORSE TRANKS WHEN I TASTE THEM!
FOR MY SHOW-AND-TELL I BROUGHT SEVEN ZITS!
LAUGH!— I THOUGHT I'D DIE!
BOY! DID I SCREW UP AEROBIOTICS!
HEY, LET'S GO PISS ON THE ROACH HIVE...
THE MENSTRUAL PERIOD WAS WHEN THERE WERE LOTS OF TROUBADOURS...
LIKE DONOVAN?
I GOT AN "A"
LOOK, MAMA... I DID IT ON MY DIPLOMA!
IT'S NOT FUNNY!
MY WEEKLY READER!
NOT GRITS AGAIN!
HAW! HAW!
"IN THE SPLIT SECOND THAT FOLLOWED, MY ENTIRE LIFE FLASHED BEFORE MY EYES..."
"WHO'S THE LEADER OF THE CLUB THAT'S MADE FOR
OH, GOD. CHANGE CHANNELS!
THE EARTH IS THE LORD'S AND THE FOOLISHNESS
ULTIMATELY, LIFE IS TRAGIC!
POOT!
EXCUSE ME
5

"...THEN I HEARD MY BONES CRACKLING..."
KA-POP!
"...MY VEINS SPLITTING..."
THUP! GURGLE!
PCHING! PCHING! PCHING!
"...MY MOLECULES DISENGAGING..."
"...ALONG WITH VARIOUS UNIDENTIFIABLE LIQUID NOISES..."
GLURCH!
"...AND THEN THE CHAOS SPLIT LIKE A CURTAIN–AND I SAW—"
ROACH HEAVEN
BUCKY BUG–RSD. MGR.
ROACH HEAVEN!
FAR OUT!
"...AND AT THE TOP OF IT ALL WAS THE BIG, BLACK MOTHER COCKROACH OF ALL MOTHER COCKROACHES..."
"...ROACH HEAVEN RISING UP BEFORE ME!"
6

"THE VIRGIN GLADYS!"
HAVE YOU BEEN WASHED IN THE BLOOD OF THE LAMB, MY CHILD?
"THINKING FAST, I AD-LIBBED A RESPONSE..."
NO–BUT I USED TO GO SKINNY DIPPING IN THE PORK GRAVY, YOUR MAIDENHEAD...
"IT WAS THE WRONG RESPONSE..."
PORK?!
PORK?!
PORK?!

'PORK?' SHE GASPED IN FURY!
SUDDENLY, THUNDER ROLLED... THE CLOUDS OPENED UP BENEATH ME, AND...

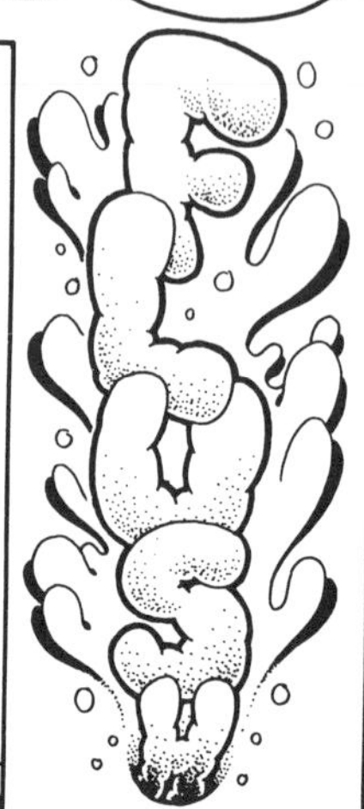

WHAT HAPPENED, TUSSY?

I'VE JUST FOUND A FAMILIAR CRACK IN THE WOOD-WORK, GANG...

...WHICH LEADS THROUGH THE WALL TO AN OBSCURE CRANNY IN A CERTAIN CLOSET...

...THE VERY CLOSET WHICH IS STILL THE LAIR OF A PARTICULARLY NEFARIOUS ITEM OF FOOTWEAR...

AND SO, MY FRIEND...WE MEET AGAIN!
GRONK!?
7

SQUASH ME, WILL YOU?–YOU FUCKING SHOE!
CLUMP!
CLUMP!
CLUMP!
TUSSY, WAIT!
YOU MUSTN'T TAKE THE LAW INTO YOUR OWN HANDS!
HA! NOW YOU'RE CORNERED!
GRONK!
IT'S INHABITED!
FWAP!
GULP! SWALLOW!
GRONK!
GOSH!...
ARE YOU THERE, AUNT TUSSY?
BELCH!
GODDAMN FROG!
OH...OF COURSE!
MY UMBRELLA, PLEASE...
THANK YOU!
I'LL BE BACK LATER WITH REINFORCEMENTS!
BONK!
8

THAT'S AN EIGHT-STORY DROP!
GIVE OR TAKE A CHAPTER...

SMUSH!

OOO! THAT BUS IS GONNA NEED A PAINT JOB!

WELL, AT LEAST SHE GOT RID OF THAT OBNOXIOUS FROG!
YEAH! NOW WE CAN GET AT THOSE COOKIES IN THE CLOSET!
RIGHT ON!

SAY...IT'S MORNING, ALREADY...
I'D BETTER GET BUSY!
IMPORTANT MEETING TODAY

LET'S SEE NOW... WHAT WAS THAT MEETING FOR?

OH, YES...A DISCUSSION GROUP ON THE THEOLOGICAL IMPLICATIONS OF ROACH HEAVEN AND HOW THE HELL WE'RE GOING TO GET INTO THE JOHN THAT TUSSY LEFT LOCKED!

THERE! ONE OF MY MOST INSPIRED AGENDAS!

EVERYBODY OUT!
IT'S TIME FOR THE MEETING!

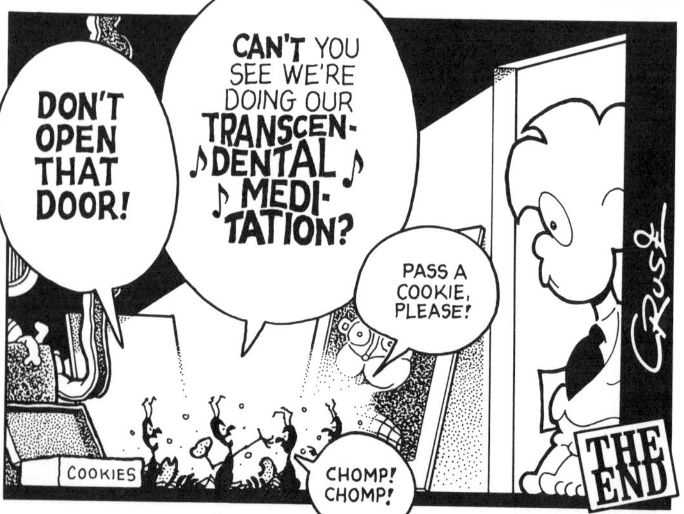
DON'T OPEN THAT DOOR!
CAN'T YOU SEE WE'RE DOING OUR TRANSCEN-DENTAL MEDI-TATION?
PASS A COOKIE, PLEASE!
COOKIES
CHOMP! CHOMP!
CRUSE
THE END

BAREFOOTZ
by Howard Cruse

in

HINT & RUN

GOSH, I'D LIKE TO VISIT LONGER, DOLLY -BUT I'VE GOT A DATE TONIGHT!
Crunch! Crunch!

I GUESS I'D BETTER START CLEANING UP!...

I HOPE YOU'LL BE ABLE TO COME VISIT ME AGAIN VERY SOON!
Crunch! Crunch!

Crunch! Crunch!

Crunch! Crunch!

MAYBE SHE'S GETTING HARD OF HEARING...

Crunch! Crunch!
1

Crunch!
Crunch!

Crunch!
Crunch!

Crunch!
Smack!
Crunch!

Crunch!
Crunch!

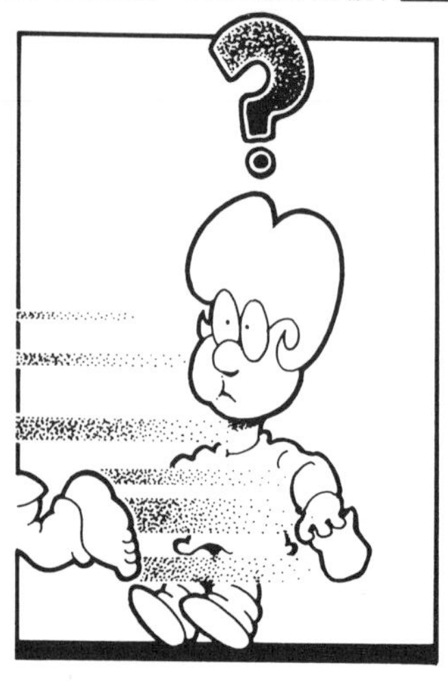

Crunch,
Crunch??

LOOKS LIKE SHE'S FINALLY **LEFT!**

LET'S SEE... WHERE ARE MY **KEYS?**

I HOPE I'M NOT **LATE!**

Crunch!
Crunch!

CRUSE
I DON'T THINK HE'S GOING TO INVITE ME **ALONG...**
CLICK!
THE END

YOUR FRITZI IS REALLY A NIFTY CAT, HEADRACK!
A LITTLE ON THE DUMB SIDE, THOUGH...
BAREFOOTZ
by Howard Cruse

IT TAKES HER FOREVER TO PICK UP ON THE SIMPLEST THINGS!

NO, FRITZI! NOT THERE!
YOU KNOW BETTER THAN TO DO THAT THERE!

THE BATHROOM IS THAT WAY!

©1977 by H. Cruse

SHE SEEMS PRETTY WELL-TRAINED TO ME!
YEAH-BUT IT TOOK ME SIX WEEKS TO GET THE IDEA ACROSS TO HER!

STILL...I DON'T THINK YOU HAVE ANYTHING TO COMPLAIN ABOUT...

SOME CATS NEVER LEARN TO SHED IN THE JOHN!
CRUSE

I HOPE YOU'RE **HUNGRY,** HEADRACK—'CAUSE I'VE REALLY WHIPPED UP A **FEAST!**
BAREFOOTZ
by Howard Cruse
HUNGRY?! I'M **STARVING!**

SAY, **FELLAS!** BAREFOOTZ HAS MADE SOME OF THAT **STICKY STUFF!**
I **LOVE** PLAYIN' IN **STICKY STUFF!**
STICKY STUFF!
WOW!
ME **FIRST!**
LOOK! HERE'S SOME **GUMMY STUFF,**
...AN' SOME RED 'N' GREEN **FLIPPERY THINGS!**
WHEE!
SMUSH! SPLOOSH!

SEE HOW IT STICKS TO MY **DROOPSIES?**
YIK!
JOEY! **STOP** THAT!
SLOOP! SLOOP!
WHAT'S GOING **ON?**
IT'S A **'STICKY PARTY'**
DON'T POOT IN TH' **MIDDLE** OF IT!
I WAS ONLY GONNA **KICK** IT!
GIGGLE!
FLOP! SLURP! STOMP! SPLUDGE! GURGLE!

HEY, **GANG!** WE'VE GOT **COMPANY,** Y'KNOW...

COMPANY?
OH, GOLLY...
EXCUSE US!
WE'RE SORRY!
OOPS!

THEY **KNOW** NOT TO DO THAT WHEN **COMPANY'S** HERE!
CRUSE

©1987 by H. Cruse
BAREFOOTZ
by Howard Cruse
SAY, LOOK WHAT IT SAYS HERE IN THIS BOOK!
THAT'S VERY INTERESTING!
I CAN'T WAIT TO SURPRISE THE ROACHES!

GUESS WHAT I'M PLANNING TO WHIP UP FOR SUNDAY DINNER, GANG!

JELLIED OYSTERS?
VENISON SOUFFLÉ?
NOPE...
TURNIPS UNDER GLASS?
HOT STONED CRABS?
FLAMINGO BALLS?
KUMQUATS AU GRATIN?

BOILED MOOSE!

BOILED MOOSE?!!
YECCH!
ARE YOU KIDDING?

THEY'RE STRINGY AND GREASY!
THEY TASTE LIKE MINCED CAMEL CRUD!
THEY'RE ALL MUSHY INSIDE!
THEIR DRUMSTICKS ARE PIGEON-TOED!
THEY STICK TO YOUR FINGER-NAILS!
THEIR NOSES DRIP!

O.K... WELL, LET'S JUST FORGET IT, THEN!

...BESIDES, THEIR ANTLERS ALWAYS GET STUCK BETWEEN YOUR TEETH!
I DON'T GET IT, DOLLY! THAT BOOK SAYS THAT COCKROACHES LOVE BOILED MOOSE!
NO, YOU READ IT WRONG... IT SAYS MOOSES LOVE BOILED COCK-ROACHES!
...BUT ONLY PLATONICALLY!
Toke! Toke!
CRUSE
Drawn for Myron

GOD! I'M SO **HORNY** TODAY!

I WISH **BAREFOOTZ** WAS HERE!

BAREFOOTZ

by Howard Cruse

I DON'T KNOW... IF HE **WAS** HERE, I'D ONLY BE **FRUSTRATED!**

MAYBE IF I COULD JUST HEAR HIS **VOICE**...

THERE'S NO LAW AGAINST A FRIENDLY, CASUAL **PHONE CALL!**

I HOPE HE CAN'T TELL WHAT A **STATE** I'M IN...

Dial Dial

CHORF! CHORF!

HELLO?

DOLLY? IS THAT **YOU?**

CHORF! CHORF!

CHORF! CHORF!

THERE'S SOME KIND OF **INTER-FERENCE** ON THE LINE!

I CAN'T **HEAR** YOU, DOLLY...

CHORF! CHORF!

OH! UH....

EXCUSE ME, BAREFOOTZ...

I'VE GOT TO **GO!**

HOW **EMBARRASSING!**

CHEWING THE **PHONE** LIKE THAT IS REALLY **BAD** FOR YOUR **TEETH!**

CRUSE

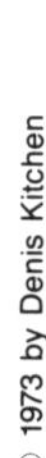

BAREFOOTZ
by Howard Cruse
HAPPY BIRTHDAY, DOLLY!
K9
WHY... BAREFOOTZ!
I BROUGHT YOU SOME CANDY!
Chocky Chompies

STRANGE THAT YOU SHOULD REMEMBER MY BIRTHDAY...
WITH MY MEMORY, I GUESS YOU'RE RIGHT!

SNIFF!

YOU DIDN'T SLIP ANY APHRO-DISIACS IN THESE, DID YOU?

OF COURSE NOT! WHY WOULD I DO THAT?

Crunch!
YOU'RE SURE YOU DIDN'T SLIP ANY APHRODISIACS IN THESE..?
POSITIVE!
Chocky Chompies
Rattle! Rattle!

THERE! YOU SEE, BAREFOOTZ?

THAT'S WHY YOU NEVER GET ANYWHERE WITH ME!

YOU NEVER LAY ANY GROUNDWORK!
CRUSE
Chocky Chompies

BAREFOOTZ
by Howard Cruse
GOOD NIGHT, DADDY...
GOOD NIGHT, DADDY...
GOOD NIGHT, STUD...
GOOD NIGHT, DADDY...
ARE ALL OF THOSE ROACH KIDS **YOURS**, CECIL?

2,769 OF THEM ARE!
...THERE'S A COUPLE OF **NEIGHBOR KIDS** STAYING OVERNIGHT WITH **LUCILLE!**

THAT'S QUITE A **FAMILY!**

YES... MARGE AND I HAVE BEEN BLESSED WITH **OFFSPRING**, ALL RIGHT!

OF COURSE, WE DIDN'T START **OUT** TO HAVE SO **MANY!**
ONE THING JUST LED TO **ANOTHER**...

STILL... THAT'S A LOT OF **MOUTHS** FOR A WORKING ROACH TO **FEED!**

LAST WEEK I TOLD MARGE WE WERE GOING TO **HAVE** TO OPT FOR **FAMILY PLANNING**...
...AND TO **HELL** WITH THE **POPE!**

HOW DOES **MARGE** FEEL ABOUT THAT?
OH, SHE'S ALL **FOR** IT...

SHE'S DOWNTOWN GETTING A COUPLE OF HUNDRED **ABORTIONS** RIGHT **NOW!**
POP!
FIZZZ
BEER
CRUSE

"...'Masterful' is not too strong a word for Mr. Cruse's fanciful excursion into anthropomorphic erotica... A volcanic erection of comedy..."
-Captain Kangaroo

"... Definitely not for the kiddies..."
-Bunny Rabbit

"... Happily free of Cruse's usual tortured metaphysics... this tender tale offers a meaty treat for the horny businessman..."
-Mr. Green Jeans

"...On second thought, 'Masterful' is too strong a word..."
-Captain Kangaroo

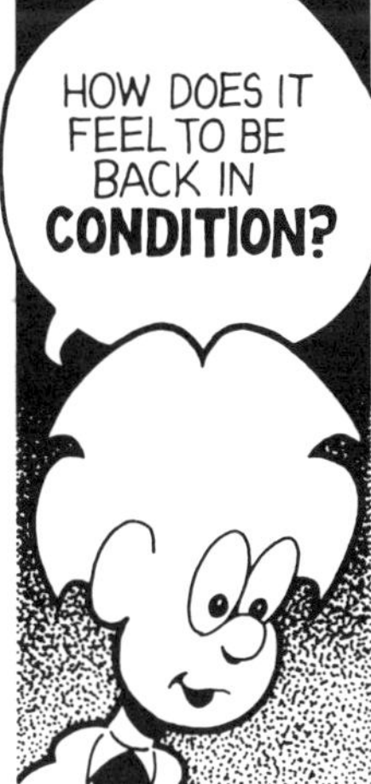

Whappity Whappity Whappity Whappity
LORDY!

YOU SWING A MEAN JUMPROPE, THORNTON!

JUST RE-CHARGING THE OLD FOOT-WORK, BABY...
I THOUGHT HE WAS A LAWN MOWER!
THE DOOR..?
KNOCK! KNOCK!

THAT MUST BE HEADRACK!

MISSION ACCOMPLISHED!

I GOT YOU THE LAST PACKAGE OF 'NUT-POWER WHEAT-BALLS' IN THE STORE!

WHAT KIND OF CEREAL IS THIS?
IT'S THE LATEST THING IN BREAKFAST ENERGY FOOD!
IT'S GOT SO MUCH PROTEIN, YOU CAN EAT IT WITH CATSUP!
THE T.V. ADS SAY THAT IT PICKS YOU UP, KEEPS YOU GOING, BRIGHTENS YOUR OUTLOOK DOUBLES YOUR HORSEPOWER, FIGHTS IRREGU-LARITY...
...GIVES YOUR TEETH SEX APPEAL AND STIMULATES THE FLOW OF VITAL HORMONES!
OF COURSE, THEY MAY BE PAID TO SAY THAT...

YOU MUST HAVE A HEAVY DATE TONIGHT!
OH, IT'S NOT FOR ME!

IT'S FOR THORNTON AND VERANDA!

YOU MEAN THE ROACHES?
SHH!
CAN I HAVE A GLASS OF WA-WA?
2

WHAT YOU WANT IS 'WATER,' VERANDA... NOT 'WA-WA!'
ACTUALLY, WHAT I WANT IS BOURBON AND WA-WA!

VERANDA'S BEEN HITTING HER SECOND CHILDHOOD RECENTLY!
I THOUGHT SHE WAS ALREADY IN HER FOURTH ONE!

SHE REGRESSED!
TAP WA-WA YIK!

THERE'S NOTHING WRONG WITH TAP WATER, VERANDA!
NOTHING A LITTLE BOOZE WOULDN'T KILL!

HEY IN THERE... WHAT ABOUT MY WATER??
WOULD YOU MIND TAKING THORNTON HIS WATER?
IN A WATERING PAIL?
THERE'S NO RESPECT FOR THE AGED!

HE WON'T USE THE REGULAR SHOWER...
WHAT WITH ATHLETE'S FOOT RAMPANT, HUH?

YOU AND VERANDA ARE REALLY GOING IN FOR THE CALIS-THENICS, -EH, THORNTON?
SHAMPOO

SOUNDS LIKE A LOT OF HASSLE TO ME!
♪

DO COCKROACHES ALWAYS GO TO THIS MUCH TROUBLE?
...PRIOR TO SCREWING, I MEAN!

LISTEN, SONNY... HOW OLD DO YOU THINK I AM?

I'LL TELL YOU... 152!

GOSH... YOU DON'T LOOK 152...
...AND VERANDA IS 187!
3

I GUESS WHEN YOU'RE **THAT** OLD, THINGS DON'T COME AS **EASILY**...
YOU'RE DURN **TOOTIN'!**

-UNLESS YOU'RE IN **SHAPE!**
-UNLESS YOU HAVE THE **VIGOR** TO **SUBDUE** THE WILD **SHE-BEAST**...
WHAM!

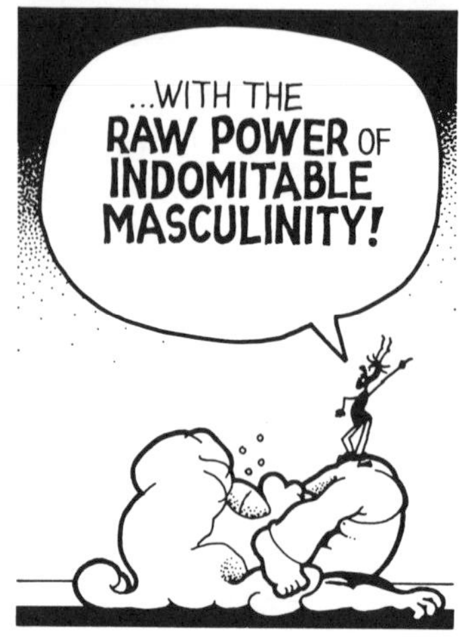
...WITH THE **RAW POWER** OF **INDOMITABLE MASCULINITY!**

-ALL THE WHILE MAINTAINING THE OBLIGATORY CIVILITIES OF **SECURITY** AND **ROMANCE!**...

SUBDUED **LIGHTS**...
GENTLE **MUSIC**...
A HINT OF **MATRIMONY** IN THE AIR...

...PLUS THE SUPPORTIVE ENCOURAGEMENT OF **FRIENDS** AND **NEIGHBORS**...
...WHICH IS WHY WE HAVE **CHEER-LEADERS!**
GET IT UP! GET IT ON! GET IT IN LOW! TAKE A DIP AN' LET 'ER RIP! GO, TEAM, GO!

GOSH...IT'S NICE TO SEE REAL **COMMUNITY INVOLVEMENT** AGAIN!

WELL, THIS IS NO **LIASON** TO TAKE **LIGHTLY** **-IS** IT, GANG..?
SHIT, NO!....
THEY'RE THE CREAM OF THE GENES! THE TIP OF THE TOP! THE KING AND THE QUEEN OF THE PICK OF THE CROP!
TEAM
4

YOU MEAN—YOU AND VERANDA WERE...
...CHOSEN SCIENTIFICALLY FOR GENETIC MOXIE!

OUR OFFSPRING WILL BE A 'SUPER-ROACH'...
IMMUNE TO PESTICIDES!
IMMUNE TO DISEASE!
...AND MOST OF ALL...
—IMMUNE TO THE VERY LIGHTNING ITSELF!

...IMMUNE TO GLORY!!
'Glory'-who lives Under the Bed-is a Natural Enemy to Cockroaches!

NAUGHTY, NAUGHTY, VERANDA!

WE DON'T SNEAK INTO BAREFOOTZ'S LIQUOR CABINET WHILE BAREFOOTZ ISN'T LOOKING!
I WAS ONLY SMELLING IT...

THINK OF ALL YOUR FRIENDS WHO ARE COUNTING ON YOU...

WE WANT VERANDA!
WE WANT VERANDA!
YOU CAN'T LET DOWN YOUR PUBLIC!

MY PUBLIC! IT'S CALLING TO ME..

THERE SHE IS!...
I AM YOURS!
THAT'S THE SPIRIT!
5

I WANT HER AUTY-GRAPH!
NO, I WANT HER AUTYGRAPH!
ME FIRST!
NO, ME!
I WANT IT!
GOOD LORDY MERCY!
SHE'S RUNNING AWAY!
STOP HER!
WAIT, VERANDA
COME BACK!
SAY, GANG... LET'S KEEP A REIN ON OUR ENTHUSIASMS!
IS VERANDA READY?
YEAH... WHERE IS THE SEXY LITTLE SUGAR BLOSSOM?
SHE'S IN THERE MEETING HER PUBLIC!
GET BACK, SWINE!
I GOT A EYE LASH!
I GOT A TOENAIL!
I TOUCHED THE HEM OF HER GARMENT!
AWAY, PHILISTINES!
THAT WASN'T NO GARMENT, DODO!
I THINK THE CHEER-LEADERS NEED TO BE ORGANIZED, HEADRACK...
I THINK YOU'RE RIGHT!
...NOW DO I HEAR NOMINATIONS FOR VICE-PRESIDENT?
POINT OF ODOR!
I SECOND THE QUESTION!
I THIRD THE SECOND!
CAN I BE EXCUSED?
I NOMINATE MY MAMA!
POINT OF ARDOR!
POINT OF UDDER!
SHE'S ALREADY PRESIDENT!
I MOVE WE TABLE THE PRESIDENT!
ARE YOU GUYS SET TO GO?
DURN TOOTIN'...
LET'S GET IT OVER WITH!
READY WITH THE MUSIC?
SPARE US THE NATIONAL ANTHEM, PLEASE...
6

WHY DON'T WE DO IT IN THE ROAD?...
I DIDN'T KNOW DORIS DAY HAD RECORDED THIS...
READY... GET SET...
GO!

WAIT A MINUTE! SHE'S NOT WEARING A GARTER BELT!
?

I CAN'T SCREW A LADY WITHOUT A GARTER BELT!!
I WANT A GLASS OF WA-WA...

I'D BETTER HAVE A LITTLE TALK WITH HIM!

WHAT KIND OF PERVERTED OPERATION IS THIS ANYWAY?

MAYBE YOU'D BETTER HAVE A LITTLE TALK WITH HIM!

DWIGHT AND MAMIE EISENHOWER NEVER USED A GARTER BELT!
FAR OUT!

THE ONLY CURE FOR SEXUAL IGNORANCE IS STRAIGHT FACTS!
DON'T KNOCK IT TILL YOU'VE TRIED IT!
WELL... LIVE AND LET LIVE!
VARIETY IS THE SPICE OF LIFE!

MAKE WOOF -NOT WARP!
IF YOU ASK ME, YOU NEED TO WHIP UP A MORE ROMANTIC ATMOSPHERE, BAREFOOTZ!
7

WHY DON'T YOU TELL US A ROMANTIC STORY?
I DONT KNOW ANY ROMANTIC STORIES!
MAYBE I COULD BUY ONE...
I'LL CHECK OUT OUR FRIENDLY NEIGHBORHOOD ROMANTIC STORY STORE!
NO ONE UNDER 21 ADMITTE
Books • M

THIS LOOKS PROMISING...
LET'S SEE YOUR I.D., BUDDY!
DINGY DONGS
GONAD THRILLS
DOPEY DILDO COMIX
PASTY DONGS
STICKY RICKS
DORKY DOINGS
HORNY HUMPS
CRUSTY BUSTS
LUSTY BUSTS
BUSTY LUST
BALLSY BOOBS

WHERE'S BAREFOOTZ?
HE'S TRYING TO FIND VERANDA!
Toke! Toke!

VWOP!

CHEERS?
GLOOP!

ATTENTION, EVERYONE!
HONEST... I WAS ONLY SMELLING IT AND IT WENT OFF!

HEADRACK IS GOING TO READ US A BEDTIME STORY!
WHEE!
YIPPEE!
EAT YOUR HEART OUT, UNCLE REMUS...
DIG IT!
OH BOY!
A STORY!
Glug! Glug!
8

CHAPTER ONE: "Do it to me!" said cute blonde co-ed Jill Bulging as she winked at her muscular faculty counselor Jack Wellhung in the cafeteria. Without a word the handsome Celtic Dialects professor flung his lunch tray to the floor, tore the garments from her lush body and discarded his own academic garb as primal urges obliterated his customary professorial diffidence..."
HIC!
GONAD THRILLS
"Their naked bodies merged rhythmically amid the damp salad and the hot gravy that glistened on the floor beneath them..."
"Her tongue wove a moist path through the tight curls of his chest hair..."
MY LORD! HE'S STARTING TO SLOBBER!
"With sensual impude
his fingers explor
the forbidden po
that sheltered he
THE OLD CODGER'S COMING DOWN WITH RABIES!!
"Soon the very salt of their perspiration began to throb with anticipation..."
DROOL!
IT'S NOT NICE TO HIDE FROM DADD-D-D-DEEEEEEEE...
WHERE ARE YOU, MY SWEET..?
SPAT!
"...as the Texas gusher of their passion sent its crude oil into the stratosphere..."
GONAD THRILLS
HA!
SMUNCH!
"Meanwhile, Prudence Glintz was across town preparing to address the P.T.A..."
YOU CAN STOP READING NOW, HEADRACK...
I THINK WE'VE GOT THE BALL ROLLING!
GONAD THRILLS
9

WAIT A MINUTE!
WHAT ABOUT PRUDENCE GLINTZ?
WHAT ABOUT THE P.T.A.?
ACTUALLY, I WAS GETTING KIND OF INTERESTED IN PRUDENCE MYSELF...

HOW CAN YOU THINK ABOUT PRUDENCE?
LOOK AT THIS!...

FAR OUT! WHAT ARE THEY DOING IN THERE?
IT'S CALLED 'FORE-PLAY!'

LOOKS LIKE A GOOD WAY TO LOSE AN ELBOW!
WE WANT PRUDENCE!
WE WANT PRUDENCE!

FORGET ABOUT PRUDENCE!

IT'S HARD TO FORGET A REALLY WELL-DRAWN CHARACTER...
BUT THIS IS AN EPOCHAL OCCASION!

THORNTON AND VERANDA WILL BE GOING DOWN IN HISTORY!

I WONDER IF HISTORY IS READY FOR THIS!
NEVER AGAIN WILL GLORY CONTROL THE DESTINY OF ROACHDOM...

TODAY SHOULD BE A DAY OF JUBILATION AND REJOICING!

COME ON, CHEERLEADERS... LET'S HAVE SOME ENTHUSIASM!!
♪ DECK THE HALLS WITH BOUGHS OF HOLLY... ♪
PSSST!
10

YOU PSSSTED?
WE'RE READY FOR OUR NUT-POWER WHEAT-BALLS!

THEY'RE READY FOR THEIR NUTPOWER WHEATBALLS!!

DID YOU ROACHES HEAR THAT?...
??- WHERE DID THEY GO??

STICK 'EM IN! LICK 'EM UP! SWEETEN YOUR JUICE! NUTPOWER WHEATBALLS MAKE-UM PAPOOSE!
I'M BEGINNING TO FEEL LIKE A FATHER MYSELF!
SUGAR
NUT-POWER WHEAT BALLS

WOULD YOU LIKE A LITTLE SUGAR WITH THIS, THORNTON?
O.K. SQUAD- BACK TO THE BLEACHERS!
I'M COUNTING ON IT! (HEH! HEH!)
SIGH!
SUGAR

YOU TWO ARE GONNA LOVE THIS CEREAL...
IT'S REALLY DYNAMITE!
SPLOOG

SNAP! CRACKLE! BOOM!
ALSO... IT'S VERY CRISP!
ARE YOU KIDS READY TO DIG IN?
LET'S GO, VERANDA!

DON'T WOLF YOUR FOOD, NOW...
11

HOW'S IT GOING?
THEY'RE WOLFING THEIR FOOD!
GLORCH! GLORCH!

COULD WE HAVE A LITTLE CATSUP, PLEASE..?

ALSO SOME BOURBON AND WA-WA!
WITH-OUT THE WA-WA!

PLUS SOME SAUER-KRAUT AND FRENCH DRESSING.......
.......MAYONNAISE, GRITS, PEANUTS, FRIED RICE, CHOPPED PICKLES AND A DASH OF SALT—THEN STIR US WELL, TOP US WITH COCO-NUT AND BAKE US IN THE OVEN FOR 20 MINUTES AT 350°...
...OR UNTIL BROWNED!
INSTANT GRITS
RICE

MMMM... IT'S SO SQUISHY IN HERE...
LET NO ONE DENY THAT JULIA CHILD HAS HAD HER IMPACT ON THE SEXUAL REVO-LUTION!

MMM!
OHHH!
OOO!
AHHH!
DO IT AGAIN WITH THE MARMALADE, LOVER...

TIMER
PING!

ARE YOU GUYS ALL DONE?

OH, NO!

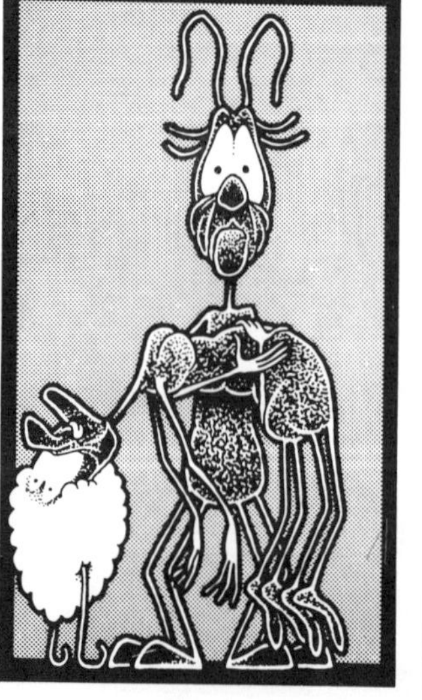

IS SHE..?
I DON'T THINK HER HEART COULD TAKE IT!
12

THAT WASN'T MY **HEART** YOU WERE **STICKIN'** IT TO!
THE SLOW WEEKS PASS... THE 'STORK' APPROACHES...
I SURE COULD GET INTO A **PEAT MOSS SANDWICH** RIGHT NOW...
KNOCK! KNOCK!

HAVE YOU SEEN THE **NEWSPAPER?**
XAMINER
EROUS

NUTPOWER WHEATBALLS HAVE BEEN **BANNED!**

THESE DOCTORS SAY THAT THEY CAUSE **BIRTH DEFECTS!**
XAMINER
EROUS

OH...THEY'RE PROBABLY **EXAGGERATING!**

YOU KNOW HOW IT IS WHEN **DOCTORS** START **SCARING** EACH OTHER...
BAREFOOTZ!
IT'S **HERE,** BAREFOOTZ!
IT'S **HERE!**
-VERANDA JUST HAD HER **BABY!**

I'VE HEARD OF **DEFORMED BABIES** BEFORE...
...BUT A **FROG?!**
GRONK!
SIGH!
STEP RIGHT UP, LADIES AND GENTLEMEN...
15¢
"... A dénouement to stagger the imagination..."
-Mr. Moose
CRUSE
THE END

IT ALL FITS!
BAREFOOTZ
by Howard Cruse
LOOKS LIKE A STORM's COMING UP, DOLLY...
WHAT'S REALLY FANTASTIC, BAREFOOTZ, IS HOW IT ALL FITS!

WE'D BETTER HEAD FOR SHELTER!
IS IT GOING TO RAIN?

THIS TREE SHOULD KEEP US DRY!
I HOPE MY HAIRDO DOESN'T GET RUINED!

?
CRACK!

THAT LIGHTNING HIT KIND OF CLOSE, DIDN'T IT?
LOOK WHAT IT DID TO THAT TREE!

BLAM!
1

GOSH! IT'S UNUSUAL FOR LIGHTNING TO STRIKE **TWICE** IN ONE....

...PLACE!...
WHAM! CRACKLE! CRUNCH!

THIS MUST BE SOME SORT OF **MAJOR ELECTRICAL ZONE!**

LOOK, BAREFOOTZ!
THAT BIG **TREE** HAS BEEN COMPLETELY **DESTROYED** –BUT THE LITTLE **FLOWER** BESIDE IT HAS MIRACULOUSLY **SURVIVED!**

GOD MUST REALLY ***LOVE*** **FLOWERS!**

ON THE OTHER HAND, THE BIG **TREE** GETS TO GO ON UP TO **HEAVEN**...

...WHILE THE **FLOWER** HAS TO STAY HERE AND GET **RAINED** ON!

BAM!

–WHEREAS **OUR** TREE'S GOTTA STICK AROUND FOR THE **RAIN**...
...WHILE OUR **FLOWER'S** ALREADY MADE IT TO **HEAVEN!**

I GUESS IT ALL **FITS!**
YEAH...I GUESS IT ALL **FITS!**

IT'S A GOOD THING WE DIDN'T STAND UNDER **THAT** TREE...
...OR WE'D BE GETTING **DRENCHED**
Boy! Was I thirsty!
KRUSE
THE END

HEY, BAREFOOTZ... TELL US A SCARY STORY!
BAREFOOTZ
by Howard Cruse

I DON'T KNOW ANY STORIES!
SURE YOU DO!
YOU CAN MAKE ONE UP!
WELL...I GUESS I COULD TRY...
OH, BOY!

HE'S GONNA TELL US A STORY!
JUST SETTLE DOWN, O.K.?
BE SURE IT'S REALLY CREEPY!

I'M SO EXCITED
QUIET IN BACK, PLEASE!
I'M GETTING SCARED AL-READY!
MY STOMACH HURTS!
UK! UK!

LET'S SEE, NOW...

THE SKY WAS BLACK...

THE FULL MOON WAS ROUND...

AN OWL HOOTED IN A TREE...

THE TROUBLE WITH HIS STORIES IS... THEY DON'T LEAVE ANYTHING TO THE IMAGINATION!
CRUSE

BAREFOOTZ
by Howard Cruse
SAY... HERE'S AN INTERESTING SOUTH AMERICAN RECIPE!
COOK BOOK
Toke! Toke!

YOU TAKE A COUPLE OF DOZEN COCKROACHES AND BAKE THEM IN COFFEE BEANS AND HONEY...
Toke! Toke!

...AND THEN YOU GRIND THEM WITH FLOUR TO MAKE WHEATCAKES!

SOUNDS PRETTY TASTY!

I'D SAY IT'S TIME TO TRANSPLANT TH' PARTY!
RIGHT ON!

AM I MAKING YOU TWO NERVOUS?

I'M ONLY TELLING YOU WHAT'S DOWN HERE IN BLACK AND WHITE!
THERE'S NO POINT IN EVADING THE TRUTH!

YOU MIGHT AS WELL CONFRONT EXISTENCE AS IT IS!
...THIS IS THE ONLY WORLD WE'VE GOT!

WHATEVER HAPPENED TO ESCAPIST COOKBOOKS?
TOO BAD WE'RE OUT OF HONEY...
COOK BOOK
CRUSE

♪
BAREFOOTZ
by Howard Cruse
Fizzo the Roach is having a bad LSD trip...
IF I CAN ONLY MAKE IT TO THE BEDROOM, I'LL BE SAFE!
BUT HOW CAN I GET THERE WITH THAT CHAIR WATCHING ME?
WHY IS HE SMILING AT ME? WHAT DOES HE KNOW..?
THIS IS RIDICULOUS!
I'M NOT A CHILD... I'M A GROWN ROACH!
I CAN GO WHERE I WANT TO...
...AND I WANT TO GO IN THE BED-ROOM!
HE'S GOING TO TRY SOMETHING ...I CAN TELL!
THIS IS MY LAST CHANCE...
YAAAAAAAAAH!
SAFE AT LAST!...
I AM MASTER OF MY FATE!
DID I HEAR GLORY..?
SOMEBODY BETTER RE-UPHOLSTER THAT KID BEFORE THE MONSOON SETS IN!
CRUSE

Dear Dr. Graham,
As one of your most devoted fans, I would like to say that you are one sexy evangelist.

When I see you on t.v. I want to gather your pink body into my fuzzy purple tentacles and bathe your curly hair in my boiling saliva.

At night I dream that your vibrant genitals are throbbing within the surging green juices of my passion.

Perhaps when we meet in paradise, it shall come to pass.

Sincerely yours, GLORY

BAREFOOTZ

by Howard Cruse

UH-OH!

GRONK!

BAREFOOTZ
by Howard Cruse
ARE YOU AWAKE YET, GLORY?

WHAT WOULD YOU LIKE FOR BREAKFAST?

ANYTHING BESIDES RAISIN TOAST?

HOW ABOUT CINNAMON ON THAT TOAST?

RIGHT! WITH LOTS OF CHEESE...

...AND APPLE MINT JELLY ON TOP OF THE CHEESE!

GLORY'S GETTING SO PICKY THESE DAYS!

WE'RE ALL OUT OF APPLE MINT!

DON'T MAKE FROGS AT ME, GLORY!
GRONK! GRONK! GRONK!

I DON'T KNOW WHY I GO TO SO MUCH TROUBLE...

...SHE ALWAYS TRANSUBSTANTIATES IT BEFORE SHE EATS IT, ANYWAY!
VORP!
CRACKLE!
FIZZZZZ
CRUSE

About "Suffering Celeste"

Excerpt from a 1986 *Comics Journal* interview conducted by Steve Ringgenberg

RINGGENBERG: . . . *In one strip you did have* [Barefootz] *meeting a woman and going through a whole sexual trip.*
CRUSE: That's true.
RINGGENBERG: *That was the one where the girl brought him in and said that everything was being televised. I forget the name of the strip . . .*
CRUSE: It's called "Suffering Celeste," and it's never been published.
RINGGENBERG: *That was never published? It was one of the funnier ones, I thought.*
CRUSE: It was a mindfuck strip, a what-is-reality? strip. I had just drawn that strip in 1973 when the bottom fell out of the underground comix field. . . .The reason I didn't include "Celeste" when I finally got around to putting together *Barefootz Funnies* was that I had become aware that parts of it might come across as sexist.
RINGGENBERG: *Like the bit where Barefootz loses his temper and pins Celeste to the wall with a chair?*
CRUSE: That's Barefootz's only little moment of [machismo], and it's quickly undermined. And the fact is, it was *satirizing* machismo. Barefootz wasn't being himself; he was playing a role, he thought, for television. He was playing the role of Ramrod. But the fact that Celeste responded positively to his violence, that it got her hot, was something that I realized wasn't going to go over too well in some circles.

It would've been a different matter if I thought women would be wrong to be annoyed. But, despite my good intentions when I drew it, [when I had a chance to publish it] I wasn't at all sure they'd be wrong. If this thing ever crops up in some kind of *Barefootz* collection, I feel like I've gotta get a disclaimer on the record: Forgive me! My consciousness has been raised since I drew this!

. . .Seriously, I like many elements of that story, but there are certain things I wouldn't do the same way now.

Despite its problematic aspects, I'm including "Suffering Celeste" in this book because, of my mindfuck strips, it's probably the mindfuckingest. Even *I'm* not sure what happens in it—and I drew it!

Cruse in 1990

BAREFOOTZ

by Howard Cruse

Suffering Celeste

OOPS!

OOF!

7B
KNOCK KNOCK
I'LL PRETEND I'M NOT SHY!
HI, THERE! MY NAME IS...
THANK GOD YOU'RE HERE!
...BAREFOOTZ!
HURRY! COME INSIDE!
NOW SAY IT AGAIN!
SAY WHAT?
YOUR NAME!
BAREFOOTZ?
YOU HAVE TO SPEAK VERY DISTINCTLY...
...OR THE MICROPHONES WON'T PICK IT UP!
MICRO-PHONES?
PRETEND YOU DON'T SEE THEM!
...OR THE CAMERAS EITHER!
WHAT CAMERAS?
THE TELE-VISION CAMERAS!
I DON'T SEE ANY CAMERAS!
THAT'S BECAUSE THEY'RE HIDDEN!
I'M CERTAINLY NOT GOING TO PERFORM WITH MY PRODUCTION FACILITIES EXPOSED!
ARE YOU MAKING A T.V. SHOW?
2

HAVEN'T YOU EVER HEARD OF 'SUFFERING CELESTE'?
NO...

WELL... I'M 'CELESTE'!
FAR OUT!

AND I WANT YOU FOR MY NEW 'RAMROD'!

UH...WHAT HAPPENED TO YOUR OLD 'RAMROD'?
HE BROKE MY HEART!

HE RAN AWAY AND ELOPED WITH MY AVON LADY!

GOSH! WHY WOULD A FELLA DO THAT?
PERSONALLY, I THINK HE MARRIED HER FOR HER COSMETICS!

THOSE SOUND LIKE TOUGH SHOES TO FILL!
YOU CAN DO IT!
I'M FINISHED WITHOUT A LEADING MAN!
THEY'LL CANCEL MY SHOW!
MY CAREER WILL BE OVER!

PLEASE BE MY RAMROD, BAREFOOTZ...

...BUT I'VE NEVER ACTED ON T.V. BEFORE...
YOU'LL LOVE IT!

ALL YOU HAVE TO DO IS BE FIRM!
RAMROD HAS ALWAYS BEEN FIRM...

DON'T I NEED A **SCRIPT?**
SCRIPTS ARE FOR **AMATEURS!**
POWDER

YOU JUST WALK IN THE DOOR AND WE'LL **IMPROVISE** FROM THERE!
I'M GETTING **EXCITED!**
POWDER
PAT
PAT
PAT

WOW! **ME** ON **TELEVISION!**

I HOPE MY **MOTHER** IS WATCHING...
EVERYBODY WATCHES **'SUFFERING CELESTE'!**

REMEMBER NOW...BE **FIRM!**
7B
IT'S MY **MIDDLE NAME!**

7B
I NEVER REALIZED THAT TELEVISION SHOWS WERE SO **SPONTANEOUS!**

7B
I'LL **SURPRISE** HER WITH A JIVEY, OFF-THE-CUFF **ENTRANCE LINE!...**
WHAT'S **COOKIN',** CELESTE?

YOUR HIDE!!
?

B
K

DON'T CHANGE THE SUBJECT!
YOUR **DOUBLE-BOILER,** I PRESUME?
4

YOU REALLY OUGHT TO GO **EASY** WITH YOUR **UTENSILS,** CELESTE...
YOU'VE GOT YOUR NERVE—BUTTING INTO A **FAMILY SQUABBLE!**
I'M **DEEPLY ABASHED,** MADAME!

AFTER ALL, **POTS** AND **PANS** ARE PEOPLE, **TOO!**
...AND WHAT DO YOU HAVE TO SAY ABOUT THIS **SHIRT?**

MY **LORD!** YOU'VE BEEN **BLEEDING!**
THAT HAPPENS TO BE **LIPSTICK!**

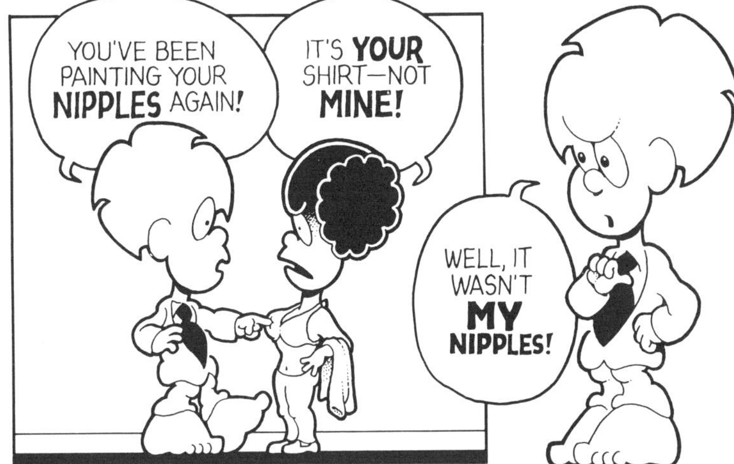
YOU'VE BEEN PAINTING YOUR **NIPPLES** AGAIN!
IT'S **YOUR** SHIRT—NOT **MINE!**
WELL, IT WASN'T **MY NIPPLES!**

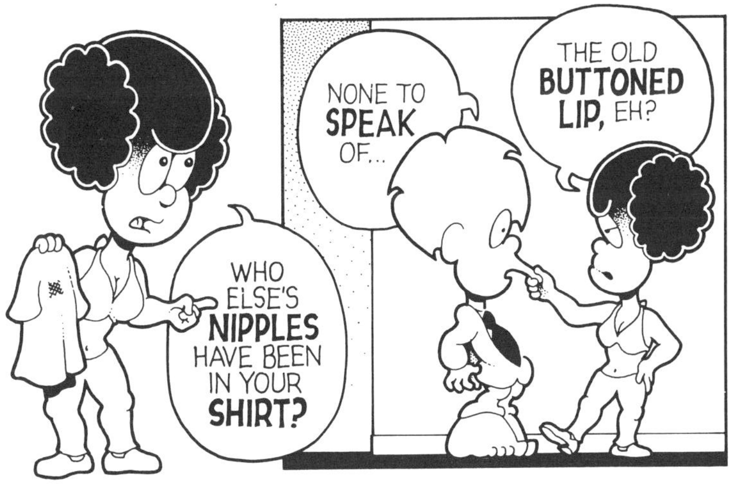
WHO ELSE'S **NIPPLES** HAVE BEEN IN YOUR **SHIRT?**
NONE TO **SPEAK** OF...
THE OLD **BUTTONED LIP,** EH?

DON'T YOU **REALIZE..?**

THIS IS WHAT'S **KILLING** US!

THE **LIES...** THE **EVASIONS...**

DO YOU THINK I **DON'T KNOW** ABOUT **MINNIE** OR **'TOOTS'...**
...OR **GWENDOLYN** OR **CHARLENE** OR **TRIXIE** OR **GEORGETTE?**

DO YOU THINK I'M **BLIND?**
WHACK!
5

NO... I'M ONTO YOUR SNEAKY TRICKS, BUDDY-BOY!
AND YOU KNOW IT!
THAT'S WHAT GIVES YOU THE KICKS—RIGHT?
ADMIT IT!
GURP!
YOU LOVE TO MAKE ME SUFFER!
YOU KNOW HOW VULNERABLE I AM....
...BUT DOES THAT STOP YOU?
HOW MANY TEARS WILL SATISFY YOU?
HOW MUCH TORTURE MUST I BEAR?
GOD KNOWS I'VE TRIED TO BE A TENDER AND LOVING WOMAN!
BUT WHAT DO I GET IN RETURN?
A BUTTON ON YOUR LIPS AND 'HELENA RUBINSTEIN' ON YOUR SOUL!
IS IT YOUR MISSION TO SEE TO MY ANGUISH?
IS THAT YOUR CALLING IN LIFE?
SKORCH
GO AHEAD! ANSWER ME!
6

WHAT ARE YOU WAITING FOR?
DO YOU WANT ME TO BLEED FOR YOU?
Tickle Tickle!
SHALL I RIP MY FLESH?
IS THAT WHAT YOU WANT?
...OR SHALL I SUFFER IN SILENCE?
I DON'T THINK I'M BEING AS FIRM AS I'M SUPPOSED TO BE!
AHEM! CELESTE, I'VE HAD ABOUT ENOUGH OF THIS DISPLAY!
TURN LOOSE OF THAT, YOU LEECH!
BOP! BOP!
YOU'VE WHAT?
ARE YOU TRYING TO GIVE ME A HARD TIME, RAMROD?
BUT I THOUGHT YOU WANTED ME TO ACT FIRM!
I DO...
...BUT I NEVER SAID ACTING WAS EASY!
OH, NO...
I WISH YOU'D RECONSIDER YOUR PLOTLINE...
OH... RATS!
I JUST THREW MY LEADING MAN OUT A 7TH STORY WINDOW!
I HOPE HE DOESN'T HURT HIMSELF!
THANK GOD FOR SOMEBODY'S CURTAINS!
7

I HATE TO DROP IN WITHOUT **PHONING**...
I'VE SEEN **YOU BEFORE!**

I'M HAVING A **DÉJA-VU!**
TELL US ABOUT IT, HONEY!
THE **GIN'S** IN THE **BATHTUB,** LOVE!
GOOD LORD! I'VE CRASHED A **BIG DO!**

WHY DON'T **I** EVER GET INVITED TO THESE PARTIES?
WELL, I **SAY**..!
?
JEEZ... WHAT'S **HIS** BAG?
ANIMAL, VEGETABLE OR MINERAL?
ORGANIC OR SYNTHETIC?
SUBJUNCTIVE OR GERUND?

HI! I'M **GIN!**
I'M **LOST!**
BUBBLE BATH

WHY DON'T YOU JUST HAVE A **SEAT**, BUDDY?
OH...UH... THANKS...

GOSH! THAT WAS **NICE** OF HIM!

I WONDER WHY HE'S GIVING HIS **CHAIRS** AWAY!

So, Ladies-wash that lipstick off your hubby's unmentionables with **Mark Spitz®** **Frozen Soap Suds...**
MARK SPITZ
SHAZAM!
BONG!
8

RAMROD! YOU SURVIVED!
WITH A CHAIR TO BOOT!

AND YOU SEEM SO CHEERFUL!
I'VE SEEN THE LIGHT, CELESTE!

YOUR SUFFERING DAYS ARE OVER!

WHAT ARE YOU SAYING?
I'M ENDING THE LIES AND EVASIONS!

I CONFESS IT ALL!

EVERYTHING YOU'VE SUSPECTED ABOUT MINNIE AND 'TOOTS' AND GWENDOLYN AND CHARLENE AND TRIXIE AND GEORGETTE IS... (SOB!)...

...IS TRUE!

SO NOW THAT HONESTY HAS PREVAILED...
...WE CAN SPEND OUR REMAINING YEARS TOGETHER IN PEACE AND HARMONY!
YOU MEAN- NO MORE LIES..?

AND NO MORE SUFFERING!
FOR ME, AT LEAST...

BUT YOURS IS JUST BEGINNING...
YOU ROTTEN TWO-TIMER!

I'M GOING TO BREAK EVERY BONE IN YOUR BODY!
NOW WAIT A MINUTE!

I KNOW YOU'RE IN CHARGE OF THE PLOT-LINE HERE...
CREAK
9

...WHICH MEANS YOU'RE IN CHARGE OF THE SUFFERING!...
YOUR SUFFERING, THAT IS...
...BUT NOT MINE!..
CRUNCH!
'CAUSE I'M NOT IN THE MOOD!
..OOF!
TOUCHÉ!
GOSH, CELESTE...
...I DIDN'T MEAN TO GET CARRIED AWAY...
YOU'RE SO MASTERFUL!
SOMEHOW IT MAKES IT ALL WORTHWHILE...
ALL THE SUFFERING... ALL THE PAIN...
JUST TO FIND ONE MAN WHO KNOWS HOW TO BE...
...FIRM!
10

I PROBABLY OUGHT TO BE RUNNING ALONG...
♪
STILL, I WOULDN'T WANT TO BREAK YOUR HEART AGAIN...
♫
OR MY STRATEGY, RAMROD..?
VORP
POK!
LET'S TURN ON THE T.V...
HOPE I DIDN'T FREAK YOU OUT WITH ALL THAT 'SUFFERING' SHIT!
OH...UH... NO... HA HA!
YOU MEAN WE'RE BROADCASTING RIGHT NOW?
SURE!
WE CAN STILL CATCH THE INSTANT RE-PLAY!
I WONDER IF MOM IS WATCHING...
I'M NOT SURE SHE'S READY FOR THIS SHOW!
11

OH, NO

THAT'S NOT US!
THAT'S AN 'I LOVE LUCY' RE-RUN!

I KNOW FRED AND ETHEL MERTZ WHEN I SEE THEM!

WHAT ARE YOU PULLING, YOU STUPID T.V. SET?

LET'S HAVE A LITTLE COOPERATION!

WHY AREN'T YOU SHOWING MY T.V. SHOW?
BONK! BONK! BONK!

WHAT'S THE MATTER WITH YOU?
BOP!

SNIFF!

IT'S O.K., BABY! ...IT WASN'T YOUR FAULT...

RICHARD NIXON IS BEHIND THIS!
MAYBE IT WAS ON THE WRONG CHANNEL!

MEANWHILE, BACK IN BAREFOOTZ'S APARTMENT...
YOU'LL NEVER GUESS WHAT WE JUST SAW ON CHANNEL 3!...
PRESTO POLISH
CRUSE
THE END

BAREFOOTZ
by Howard Cruse
THAT WAS A GREAT CAKE, DOLLY!
I'M STUFFED!
ME, TOO!
...AND WE'VE STILL GOT A SLICE LEFT OVER!
I'LL SET IT OUT FOR THE ROACHES!
WHAT'S THIS THING YOU'VE GOT FOR ROACHES?
WHY DON'T YOU STOMP ON THEM OR POISON THEM LIKE CIVILIZED PEOPLE?
I THINK I HEAR THEM COMING!
QUICK, DOLLY... HIDE OVER HERE!
Skitter! Skitter! Skitter! Skitter! Skitter! Skitter!
MUNCH! SLURP! CHOMP! GURGLE! CHEW!
THEY ENJOY THEIR FOOD SO MUCH MORE IF THEY FEEL LIKE THEY'VE SCAVENGED FOR IT!
©1973 by H. Cruse
THEY'RE REALLY KIND OF SWEET ONCE YOU GET TO KNOW THEM!
WELL, I THINK THEY'RE REVOLTING!
YUMMY!
YUMMY!
YUMMY!
YUMMY!
YUMMY!
YUMMY!
YUM YUM!
YUMMY!
YUMMY!
AND I DON'T SEE WHY YOU PANDER TO THEM...
...INSTEAD OF PUTTING THEM OUT OF THEIR MISERY!
FOR ONE THING... THEY TIP WELL!
CRUSE

YOO-HOO! COME HERE, LITTLE ROACHIE!
BAREFOOTZ
by Howard Cruse
HOW WOULD YOU AND YOUR LITTLE ROACHIE FRIENDS LIKE A BIG SURPRISE?
...A SUR-PRISE?
©1974 by H. Cruse
WHAT IS IT? WHAT IS IT?
IT WON'T BE A SURPRISE IF I TELL YOU!
...BUT IF YOU'LL SCOOT OFF AND ROUND UP ALL THE OTHER ROACHES...
...I MIGHT JUST BLOW YOUR MINDS!
THERE SHE IS! THAT'S THE LADY!
SHE'S GONNA GIVE US A SURPRISE!
HOO RAY!
IS IT BIG?
I LOVE SURPRISES!
WHERE IS IT?
WE WANT A SURPRISE! WE WANT A SURPRISE!
IS EVERYBODY READY?
YOU BET!
ZOWEE!
GET IT ON, LADY!
EVERYBODY COVER YOUR EYES NOW... AND WAIT RIGHT HERE!
SHE'S GONNA GO AFTER IT!
I'M SO EXCITED!
MY TUMMY FEELS GREEN!
GOD! THE SUSPENSE OF IT ALL!
NO PEEKING, FERDINAND!
WHAT IN THE WORLD ARE YOU DOING INDOORS WITH A LAWN MOWER, DOLLY?
CRUSE

BAREFOOTZ
by Howard Cruse
WE'VE BEEN PRETTY CLOSE FOR QUITE A WHILE, BAREFOOTZ!...
I WONDER WHY WE'VE NEVER GONE TO BED TOGETHER!
©1973 by H. Cruse
PROBABLY BECAUSE WE RESPECT EACH OTHER TOO MUCH!
NO...I DON'T THINK THAT'S IT, REALLY...
FRANKLY, I DON'T RESPECT YOU ALL THAT MUCH!
BUT I RESPECT YOU A LOT!
YOU'RE ONE OF THE MOST RESPECTABLE PEOPLE I KNOW!
I'VE RESPECTED YOU AS LONG AS I'VE KNOWN YOU...
...AND WHAT'S MORE...
...EVERY MINUTE I SPEND WITH YOU, I LEARN TO RESPECT YOU MORE!
WHATEVER I'M DOING WRONG— IT'S CUMULATIVE!
CRUSE

BAREFOOTZ
by Howard Cruse
WHY, IT'S FIZZO THE ROACH!
BAREFOOTZ?!
TEA
I HAVEN'T SEEN YOU SINCE YOU TOOK UP THERAPY!
FAR OUT!
HOW IS YOUR IDENTITY CRISIS COMING ALONG?

OH... THAT'S NO HASSLE SINCE I STARTED GETTING STONED!
TOKE! TOKE!

©1973 by H. Cruse
NOW I CAN SEE THAT SELF UNDER-STANDING IS NOTHING BUT RATIONALIZED SELF-DELUSION...

...AND THAT WHO I AM IS LESS IMPORTANT THAN WHAT I AM BECOMING!
...WHICH IS ROYALLY ZONKED!

ON THE OTHER HAND– I MAY JUST BE LAZY!...

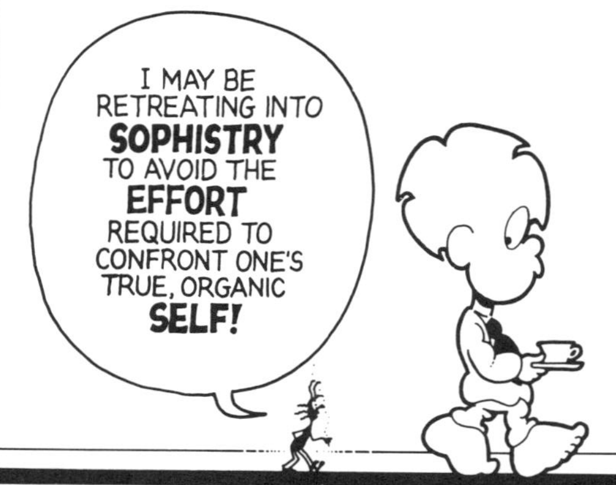
I MAY BE RETREATING INTO SOPHISTRY TO AVOID THE EFFORT REQUIRED TO CONFRONT ONE'S TRUE, ORGANIC SELF!

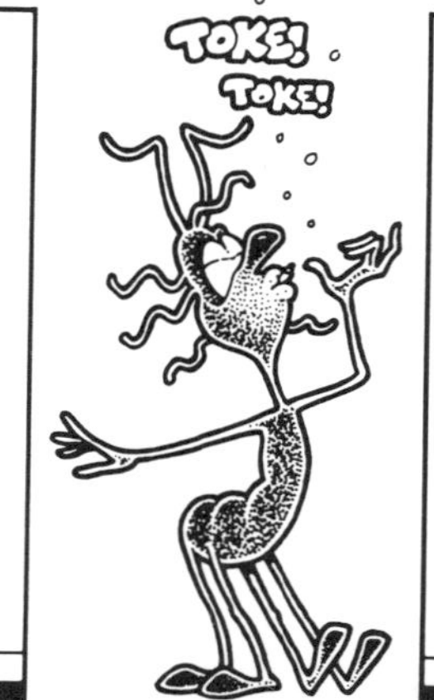
TOKE! TOKE!

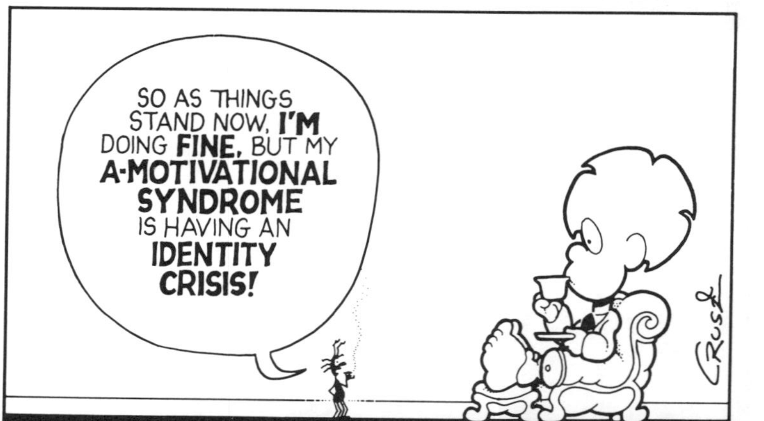
SO AS THINGS STAND NOW, I'M DOING FINE, BUT MY A-MOTIVATIONAL SYNDROME IS HAVING AN IDENTITY CRISIS!
CRUSE

BAREFOOTZ
by Howard Cruse
IS THERE ANYBODY BESIDES US IN YOUR APARTMENT, BAREFOOTZ?
NOT THAT I KNOW OF! ...WHY?
I JUST WONDERED WHY THE BATHROOM DOOR IS LOCKED!
SOUNDS LIKE THE ROACHES ARE AT IT AGAIN!
©1974 by H. Cruse
GIGGLE!
FWAP!
OOK!
SMIRK!
SPLISH!
YERK!
PWING!
CHORTLE!
IS EVERYTHING ALL RIGHT IN THERE?
TAP! TAP!
IT'S A KINKY GROUP THING THEY'VE GOTTEN INTO RECENTLY!
FRANKLY, I'M NOT SURE WHAT ATTITUDE TO TAKE ABOUT IT!
THEY LIKE TO GET TOGETHER IN A DARK BATHROOM AND POP THEIR PIMPLES ON THE MIRROR!
CRUSE

BAREFOOTZ
by Howard Cruse
You knew I had a thirst for blood when you married me, Margo...
SEE YOU LATER, GANG...
I'M GOING OUT FOR A STROLL!
NOBODY GETS INVOLVED IN TELEVISION LIKE THOSE ROACHES!
Put down that icepick, Mortimer!
I'M GETTING SCARED...
GOSH! THIS IS A CREEPY MOVIE!
I THINK I HEARD A FLOORBOARD CREAK!
...AND WE'RE HERE ALL ALONE!
SOME-THING'S TAPPING ON THE WINDOW!
THERE'S A SHADOW IN THE HALL!
IT'S MORTIMER COMING TO KILL US!
I WANT BAREFOOTZ!
ME, TOO!
MY LORD!
HELP!... BARE-FOOTZ!
WHERE ARE YOU?
SLOW DOWN, BUDDY—THIS IS A STICK-UP!
?
JUST STAY COOL AND HAND OVER YOUR BREAD, PLEASE!
I THINK I'VE GOT A QUARTER SOMEWHERE...
...AND DON'T TRY ANYTHING FUNNY!
THERE HE IS!
SAVE US, BAREFOOTZ!
YOU GOTTA STOP MORTIMER!
HE'S COMING TO GET US!
HE'S GONNA STAB US DEAD!
DON'T LET HIM KILL US!
SAVE US!
SAVE US!
SAVE US!
©1973 by H. Cruse
I HOPE YOU DON'T CONSIDER THIS FUNNY!
Cruse

BAREFOOTZ
by Howard Cruse
AN ARTIST MUST BE AN **ETERNAL OPTIMIST,** BAREFOOTZ!
HE HAS TO **BELIEVE** IN THE **PAINT** ON HIS BRUSH!
HE HAS TO BELIEVE THAT **THIS** IS THE PAINT THAT'S GOING TO MAKE HIM **FAMOUS**...
...THAT **THIS** IS THE BRUSH STROKE THAT WILL **STUN** THE **WORLD!**
OH, WELL! ANOTHER **DAY,** ANOTHER **FIASCO!**
YOU DON'T **LIKE** IT?
©1973 by H. Cruse
BLOW THE **FIRST BRUSH STROKE** AND YOU'VE **BLOWN** THE **PAINTING!**
YOU'RE NOT GOING TO THROW IT **OUT,** ARE YOU?
OF COURSE!
I CAN'T LET THE WORLD SEE MY **INFERIOR WORK!**
I THINK YOU'RE BEING TOO **CRITICAL** OF YOURSELF, HEADRACK!
OH... BUT I DON'T **MIND MY** CRITICISM...
I'M THE ONLY CRITIC WHO **LOVES** ME!
CRUSE

I'D LIKE TO **PAINT** TODAY, BUT I DON'T FEEL **INSPIRED!**
MAYBE **GLORY** COULD HELP YOU!
BAREFOOTZ
by Howard Cruse
YOU MEAN THAT **THING** THAT'S UNDER YOUR **BED?**
SURE!..SHE INSPIRES **ME ALL** THE TIME!
©1973 by H. Cruse
I FEEL KIND OF **SILLY,** BAREFOOTZ!
TAKE MY **WORD** FOR IT...YOU'LL **LOVE** IT!

FETCH ME MY OILS AND PALETTE KNIFE, IGOR!
SEE WHAT I **MEAN?**
I'VE NEVER SEEN HEADRACK SO **ANXIOUS** TO GET **HOME!**

COME ON UP AND SEE THE **PAINTING,** BAREFOOTZ!
IT'S **FINISHED ALREADY?**

IS IT EVERYTHING YOU **WANTED** IT TO BE?

IT MAY WELL BE THE MOST **MAGNIFICENT LAND-SCAPE** OF THE **20TH CENT-URY!**
IT'S GONNA BE A LITTLE HARD TO **FRAME,** THOUGH...

I GOT SO **EXCITED,** I FORGOT TO PUT A **CANVAS** ON THE **EASEL!**
I **LOVE** THE **SUNSET** ON YOUR **CANVAS-GRIP!**
Cruse

BAREFOOTZ
by Howard Cruse
HEADRACK IS HERE FOR MORE ARTISTIC INSPIRATION, GLORY!
SOMETHING COSMIC, PREFERABLY...
NOTHING'S COMING THROUGH!
REMEMBER, YOU HAVE TO LOOK HER RIGHT IN THE EYE!
©1973 by H. Cruse
THAT'S THE TICKET!
WELL... DID SHE INSPIRE YOU?
DID SHE!?
MY BRAIN IS BURSTING WITH EXPLODING VISIONS OF MYSTICAL REALMS PENETRATING THE MOST CAVERNOUS AND GLISTENING DIMENSIONS OF THE ECSTATIC IMAGINATION!
...BUT CAN MERE OILS CAPTURE THE TRANSLUCENT MAGNIFICENCE OF ETERNITY? CAN A BRUSH DEFINE THE INDEFINABLE?
WHO CAN KNOW BUT THE ARTIST??– WHO PLUNGES HIS BRUSH AS THE KNIGHT THRUSTS HIS SWORD TO CONQUER THE PROTESTING CANVAS...
CRUSE
...VANQUISHING ITS EMPTINESS TO REVEAL THE EPIC SPLENDOR WITHIN!
OF COURSE, SOMETIMES THE EXECUTION FALLS SHORT OF THE CONCEPTION!

BAREFOOTZ
by Howard Cruse
HEADRACK HAS BEEN ON SUCH A HIGH, LATELY
HE SAYS GLORY HAS BEEN INSPIRING HIM!
YEP...HE AND GLORY REALLY HIT IT OFF!
I WONDER IF GLORY WOULD MIND INSPIRING ME!...
©1973 by H. Cruse.
I DON'T SEE WHY NOT!
GOSH! THAT WOULD BE NIFTY!
WHAT DO I HAVE TO DO?
JUST TAKE A PEEK UNDER THE BED!
DOLLY COULD USE A LITTLE INSPIRATION OUT HERE, GLORY...
NO... WAIT!
YOU'RE NOT AFRAID, ARE YOU?
IT'S JUST THAT I DON'T KNOW WHAT TO EXPECT!
YOU'LL NEVER KNOW UNLESS YOU TRY, DOLLY!
I GUESS YOU'RE RIGHT!
SOMETIMES GLORY CAN OPEN UP IMPORTANT DOORS LEADING YOU TO HITHERTO UNDREAMT-OF LEVELS OF YOUR COSMIC POTENTIAL!
SHE'S LOOKING AT ME FUNNY, BAREFOOTZ...
GRONK!
OTHER TIMES, SHE JUST MAKES FROGS AT YOU...
GRONK!
GRONK!
CRUSE

BAREFOOTZ

by Howard Cruse

THE ECLIPSE

YEP! IT'S STILL **HERE!**

OF **COURSE** IT'S STILL HERE... WHERE DID YOU **THINK** IT WOULD BE?

WELL, YOU NEVER KNOW WHEN THEY MIGHT DECIDE TO **PAVE** IT!

WHAT ARE YOU LOOKING FOR?
THE STARS!
THAT'S FUNNY! THEY WERE THERE LAST NIGHT...
IT'S TOO BRIGHT FOR STARS!
THE SUN HASN'T FINISHED SETTING YET!
WELL, LAST NIGHT THEY WERE LINED UP PERFECTLY!
THERE WAS ONE THERE AND ONE THERE...
...AND ONE THERE AND ONE THERE!
...AND THAT ONLY HAPPENS EVERY EON OR SO...
...WHEN THE MOON IS ABOUT TO PASS BETWEEN THE EARTH AND THE OCEAN!
AN ECLIPSE OF THE OCEAN! WOW!
SEE? HERE COMES THE MOON!
I'M SO EXCITED!
YOU'LL SEE BETTER WITH THE TELESCOPE!
HAND IT HERE...
I WANT TO SEE IT UP CLOSE!
YOU'RE LOOKING THROUGH THE WRONG END!
OH...
2

I'VE NEVER REGRETTED JOINING THE COSMIC-EVENT-OF-THE-MONTH CLUB!
WHERE ARE WE?
RIGHT HERE!
BUT HOW DID WE GET HERE?
WE'VE BEEN HERE!
MAKE YOURSELF AT HOME! I'M GOING TO WHIP UP SOME SANDWICHES!
US, TOO!
WHIP US SOME, TOO!
I WANT PENNY BUTTER!
AWW.. COME ON, MINNIE...
THE NAVEL'S THE LIMIT, HERMIE!
Toke! Toke!
SPARE CHANGE, LADY?
GET AWAY!
UP-TIGHT!
OUTA SITE!
GET HOLD OF YOURSELF, DOLLY!
3

Come to me my Melancholy Baby...
CISTERN-LICKERS ON STRIK
BAN ROACH HIVES
CRAB LICE UNFAIR TO ORGANIZED TREE TOADS!
MAKE WOOF-NOT WARP!
IMPEDE DISRUPTIVE COUNTERPROGRESS!
FREE DILLY DALLY
Intergalactic Miscegenation NOW!
POOT!
RUBBER OVERS-UNITE!
POO POO!
Impeach Eleanor Roosevelt!
EGALIZE SPERM ARFARE
BAN SPRAY DEODORANT!

I'VE GOTTA GET OUT OF HERE!
WHO'S SHE?
DAMNED IF I KNOW!
'SCUSE ME...
I WONDER WHERE DOLLY WENT...

I THOUGHT SURE SHE'D WANT A SANDWICH!

IT TAKES ENERGY TO GET THE MOST OUT OF COSMIC PHENOMENA!

Daily Sludge
"No Comment" Snarls Coy Collie
YOU'D THINK THE PAPERS WOULD MENTION THE ECLIPSE...

WANNA BITE, PAL?
EAT AT MAUD'S
PRAISE THE LORD!
HARE KRISHNA?
SOUL FOOD!
UK!
WHAT'S SO FUNNY ABOUT ZIPPERS?
IF ONLY THEY KNEW...
CHOCOLATE-COVERED SKAG?
4

COME HERE, LITTLE PIGEON...
EVERYBODY'S INTO THEIR OWN THING!
USED BANANAS
ABORTION OR BUST

WHY ISN'T ANYBODY INTO MY THING?
WANNA BUY A CHEAP WATCH?

DOESN'T ANYBODY CARE ABOUT MY ECLIPSE?

MUST BE ONE OF THOSE 'NOUVEAU-FREAKS!'
I JUST CAN'T GET OFF ON IT, MAN...
I MEAN, WHADDAYA GONNA DO WITH A FUCKIN' ECLIPSE?
WELL...YOU CAN ALWAYS STICK IT UP YOUR ASS...
DID THEY SAY 'ECLIPSE'?

ECLIPSE?
WHAT ECLIPSE, LADY?
THE ONE RIGHT NOW!

BUT IT'S BROAD DAYLIGHT UP THERE!
IT'S NOT AN ECLIPSE OF THE SUN...

...IT'S AN ECLIPSE OF THE OCEAN!

WHAT OCEAN?
I DON'T SEE ANY OCEAN!

OF COURSE NOT...THE MOON IS IN FRONT OF IT!

SAY! I'LL BET SHE'S ON A ACID TRIP!
FAR OUT!
YEAH!
WOW!
5

CAN WE HAVE SOME ACID, LADY?
PLEEASE...
AND SOME FOR MY TEDDY BEAR, TOO..?

I HAVEN'T GOT ANY ACID! GO AWAY!
WE'VE GOTTA HAVE ACID!
OR WE'LL GO ON TO THE HARD STUFF!

...WHAT-EVER THAT IS!

CANDY STORE
"Sweets guaranteed to enrage your Dentist"
?
HOW ABOUT IF I BUY YOU SOME CANDY..?

YOU MEAN YOU'RE OFFERING CANDY TO THESE LITTLE GIRLS, LADY?

HELP! POLICE!
IT'S A CHILD MOLESTER!
CRACK!

STOP!-IN THE NAME OF THE LAW!
SHE WENT THAT WAY!
YOU DON'T SEE MANY LADY CHILD MOLESTERS!
OOPS!
I'VE NEVER MADE IT WITH AN ACID FREAK LADY CHILD MOLESTER!
IT'S A GROOVE!
FREE AT LAST!
GLURK!

MAYBE IT'S NOT A LADY!
CHUCKLE!
MAYBE IT'S A TRANSVESTYPE!
SMIRK!
YEAH...SHE LOOKS LIKE A DRAG QUEEN!
SNARF!

I HEARD THAT...
6

YEOW!
HELP!
SMASH!
WE'RE SORRY!
WE TAKE IT BACK!
YOU'RE A REAL LADY!
THAT'S BETTER!

O.K., TROOPS...
RESUME PURSUIT!

THAT'S THE TROUBLE WITH CHILD MOLESTERS!
THEY'RE SO TOUCHY!
DRAG QUEENS, TOO!!

IS THAT YOU, DOLLY?
SLAM!
LOCK!

SAY...YOU LOOK EXHAUSTED!
PANT PANT

I'VE BEEN BUSY, TOO!
OPEN UP! THIS IS THE POLICE!
PANT PANT
BAM! BAM!

I FIXED SANDWICHES AND SWEPT THE APARTMENT AND FED THE ROACHES AND WASHED THE DISHES AND READ FIFTY-THREE PAGES OF MILLARD FILLMORE'S AUTOBIOGRAPHY!
OPEN UP IN THE NAME OF THE LAW!
PANT PANT

OH!–I'LL BET YOU'RE WONDERING WHAT'S HAPPENED TO YOUR SANDWICH...
OPEN UP OR WE'LL BREAK DOWN THE DOOR!
Wheeze...
7

THE TRUTH IS: I DIDN'T KNOW WHEN YOU'D BE BACK...
...SO I GAVE IT TO GLORY!
O.K., MEN... BREAK 'ER DOWN!

I'D FIX YOU ANOTHER ONE...
...BUT I DON'T THINK THERE'S TIME!
ON THE COUNT OF 'THREE'... READY? ONE... TWO... THREE

NOPE!

ACTUALLY, I HAD A LOT MORE THINGS I WANTED TO GET DONE!

BUT THAT'S THE WAY WITH ECLIPSES...

...YOU'RE JUST GETTING INTO THEM WHEN THEY'RE OVER!

I'D SAY THIS ONE WOUND UP JUST IN TIME!
YOU'D HAD YOUR FILL, EH?

YEAH... THEY DO SEEM LONGER WHEN YOU'RE HAVING FUN!
CRUSE
THE END

An Afterword About Those Psychedelics

A young comics fan showed up at my door a few years ago. I'll call him Mark. Mark was fascinated to have discovered someone in his neighborhood who actually wrote and drew comic books. He was sharp and enthusiastic, and planned on writing comics himself.

My lover Eddie and I used to enjoy Mark's occasional visits. When he became estranged from his family and had trouble surviving, we tried to offer encouragement and counsel. But as he became absorbed into the crack culture that feeds the sidewalks of nearby Roosevelt Avenue, we learned to dread crossing paths with him.

The new version of Mark has come by a few too many times now, his hands quivering, his jawbone flexing, pleading for a "loan" until his parents come through with some money they've supposedly promised, trying to peddle stolen clothing to us. On one of his visits, a trail of feces dribbled onto our floor from the leg of his jeans.

One night Mark called from a rehab center, proud that he'd sought help as we'd urged him to. Three months later I encountered him again, wired and barely coherent. I worry that Mark is lost.

Crack makes me angry. I hate what crack has done to Mark and to others. But I also hate the use to which well-founded public apprehensions about crack and other destructive substances have been put: to intimidate into silence those of us who have fond tales to share about drugs very different from crack, drugs that liberated rather than enslaved us.

Demagogues have no use for distinctions that intrude on the popular prejudices that give them power. Their heated rhetoric quashes discussion of substances that are no more like crack than caffeine is like alcohol. Bucking the tide of today's indiscriminate anti-drug sloganeering is like trying to hold a discussion of civil liberties with a lynch mob.

Yet those of us who were part of the psychedelic scene have memories that provide us with a reality check. Some of our memories are pleasant, some unpleasant. While the drug culture of the '60s and '70s had its casualties—as do skydiving and the stresses of Harvard Law School—most of us who were there survived. Many of us feel we benefitted.

Eddie and I had dinner recently with married friends. Theirs is no hippie pad; although their home is a Manhattan apartment, these parents of a six-year-old enjoy a quiet, non-bohemian life with which most middle-class American suburbanites could easily identify.

I mentioned that I was writing this essay and spoke of how hard it has become to discuss psychedelics calmly at a time when even to hint that such chemicals might have social merit is portrayed as treasonous.

They listened, and then a small silence followed, as the couple remembered the acid trips of their own youth. They weren't remembering horror stories; they were remembering times that still made them smile, decades later.

Smiles like that (as well as grimaces spawned by recollections of anxiety-filled trips that no one would wish to repeat) are all many of us feel permitted to offer to young people today whose friends have invited them to swallow funny pills or chew on magic blotters. Their ears hear the icy admonitions of Nancy Reagan while their eyes try to interpret the misty smiles or grim shudders of people who've had the experience.

Their elders have little concrete data to offer them, because all serious research about the response of human beings to psychedelics was killed many years ago by the force of public hysteria. When we who were there do speak up, we have only anecdotes to offer a new generation. My anecdotes. Timothy Leary's. R. Crumb's. Charles Manson's. We ask the young to intelligently assess these diverse drug histories while being badgered by the moralistic snarls of drug czar William Bennett—and we hope they'll make decisions that will leave them unharmed.

At right: psychedelic drawing from 1972.

Who can draw reasoned conclusions from such an array of idiosyncratic stories? How many youngsters or young adults, correctly detecting the high bullshit content of television messages that suggest that taking any psychoactive drug will leave your brain fried like an egg, will mistakenly conclude that the messages warning them away from crack are also bullshit?

As the rewriters of history would have it, the philosophical issues raised by psychedelic drugs in the '60s were demonstrated in time to be imaginary ones propagated by a foolish generation that simply needed reining in. But in reality, those issues were never addressed. Instead they were simply drummed out of our culture's marketplace of ideas.

I couldn't have talked truthfully about my reasons for creating *Barefootz* without talking about those issues and about the connection between LSD and my artistic life in the '70s. And such issues *should* be talked about. From what I hear, psychedelics are in resurgence. That makes me uneasy. But unlike my parents' generation, I'm not frightened *of* the new acidheads—I'm frightened *for* them.

If I can draw any inferences from my own experience, psychedelics *will* be taken if they are around—if not by fad-driven masses then by a curious few. And since even if every renegade chemistry lab were busted, our nation's narcs are unlikely to succeed in wiping whole species of cacti and fungi off the face of the planet, psychedelics are likely to persist in being around.

Meanwhile, our nation, for all it righteous pretensions, is as philosophically lazy and spiritually rootless as it's ever been. Psychedelic drugs, taken in unadulterated form in appropriate settings for constructive reasons, have demonstrated a striking potential for helping human beings break through the creative blocks that have trapped them in self-defeating patterns of thought and behavior.* What's striking are the many levels on which such breakthroughs can occur, from the solution of practical or conceptual problems to profound insights about the metaphysical underpinnings of our lives. As citizens of a culture often characterized by behavior that seems morally haphazard, we should not be too quick to ban a tool that could help us regain our moorings.

There is a mountain somewhere in the U.S. with a particularly treacherous face that attracts skiers who love to take risks. When the snows fall a pilgrimage to this mountain begins. There is no ski lift there; the only way to reach the slope's top is to suffer through a laborious trek upward on foot. Every year bones are broken and spines are snapped on this slope, but the skiers still come. There is a primal need to face down that danger, and no matter how many bodies are crippled and no matter how many families or tax-supported agencies are burdened afterward with the costs of medical care, a new wave of skiers always follows the one before.

Obviously not every skier who tackles that mountain is killed or maimed. If 100 percent mortality were the test of courage, we'd have the legions of the brave skiing down the face of the Empire State Building every day. No, most skiers make it safely to the foot of the slope, having had an experience words can't describe. No explanations that any of them offer, no talk of "thrills" or "adrenaline rushes," seem profound enough to justify the risks of pain, lifelong paralysis, or even death that have been accepted as the price of a high. Yet describable or not, some profound imperative is obviously at play when these skiers look at this mountain and feel compelled to risk all.

I know about the mountain because a television news reporter did a feature on it recently. And it was clear from the tone of the correspondent's report that he looked with awe upon the daring skiers I've just described. Their bravado was obviously not for everyone, but the newsman displayed only admiration for those mad enough to seek that high. There was no finger-wagging about the possibility that hardship or grief might be inflicted on a skier's loved ones should a mishap occur. I heard no resentful tongue-clucking at the possibility that tax money might be required to alleviate the suffering of an injured skier who certainly could have stayed home and left the public coffers undisturbed.

No, there are brands of daredevilry that must always be countenanced. Safety is not the only value in life. Some adventures of the spirit are worth taking risks for. Knowing that truth, humans have walked on the moon.

---

* These observations do not spring solely from the few dozen acid trips Don and I took 20 years ago. There's a body of literature about psychedelic drugs that some of you may want to check out. The best book I've encountered recently is Jay Stevens's *Storming Heaven: LSD and the American Dream* (Atlantic Monthly Press, 1987). Not only is it useful as history, but it concludes with an extensive list of other books on the subject.

But safety is no trivial concern, and risks should be calculated, not courted mindlessly. An unprepared skier has no business on some slopes and an astronaut should understand the machine he intends to fly. When risks are assumed, there should be criteria by which an intelligent person can determine whether the terrain ahead is in fact negotiable.

Psychedelic drugs are not playtoys (though my crowd, in its youthful recklessness, did its share of treating them as such). There are real psychological hazards to assess before setting out on any journeys "to the center of the mind." People thinking about braving those hazards should be emotionally prepared and armed with accurate information about the nature of this slope they're thinking about whizzing down.

But whiz they will. Let's face facts. Just as healthy humans will express their fundamental sexuality whether or not Jesse Helms approves, people who are alienated by the soulless materialism of our day will inevitably scan the horizons for other, deeper ways of looking at life's fundamental realities. When avenues of searching for alternatives are forbidden, would-be searchers can't be faulted for looking skeptically at who is doing the forbidding, or for asking what the stake the forbidders may have in keeping the public mind under control and keeping power where it currently resides.

Unbiased scientific research on psychedelics should never have been discontinued. But it was, and George Bush isn't likely to propose a resumption of funding anytime soon. So the new generations who are poking tabs of this and blotters of that into their mouths are left to fly even more blindly than we old-timers did. The only information available to them must be ferreted out of dusty science and psychology books, out-of-date works of advocacy or condemnation, the occasional countercultural history, and the firsthand accounts, with all their limitations of perspective, of those who have traveled the drug roads before.

Those attracted to acid adventures should know about the bad trips, the bouts of paranoia, the unexpected terrors. I experienced all of those, and they weren't fun.

On the other hand, some of my most distressing tripping moments precipitated emotional breakthroughs that have contributed to my happiness in the years since. And the hallucinations—how great to remember those glorious hallucinations! Even the scary ones were luminous.

All in all, the memories of my trips—*all* the memories: the spiritual ones, the sensual ones, the hilarious or visually awe-inspiring ones—all are memories I'm happy to have tucked cozily into various crevices of my memory bank. Not that I'm inclined in my creaky middle years to scale the mountain and challenge that slope anymore. Enough is enough. I'd rather draw pictures.

Still I wonder: would I value the beautiful memories so unequivocally if I had been one of those left permanently scarred by a trip that turned mean? It's impossible to know for sure. What does the skier who is disabled on this tenth run down the mountain think about the joys of the previous nine?

No doubt it varies with the individual.

But the more truth-telling and the less sloganeering about drugs, the better. The truth will eventually surface anyway, whether the drug warriors like it or not. Suppressing truth only teaches children that their elders lie.

In talking about *Barefootz*'s genesis I've tried to be truthful. But there are many truths beyond mine. They should *all* be told, the bad stories and the good. And the people who behave as if grass equals heroin and acid equals crack and who moralize rabidly about drug use while sipping their wine, smoking their cigarettes, and smoothing out life's creases with Valium should put their rhetoric on hold long enough to ask: why is a mountain a cosmic challenge to one person when to another that same mountain is a tower of doom?

Photo: Tim J Luddy

Howard Cruse, a native of Alabama, is best known for *Wendel*, a comic strip created in 1983 for *The Advocate* and twice collected in book form (*Wendel* and *Wendel on the Rebound*). Since 1977 Cruse has lived in New York City, where he has drawn comic strips for the *Village Voice, Playboy, Heavy Metal,* and other magazines, meanwhile maintaining a presence in underground comic books such as *Snarf, Bizarre Sex*, and *Dope Comix*. In 1980 he became founding editor of *Gay Comix*. His current project is a graphic novel scheduled for publication in 1993. For the last eleven years Cruse has shared his life with Ed Sedarbaum, a book editor.